Faith, Hope, and Love

Now faith is assurance of things hoped for, a conviction of things not seen. For therein the elders had witness borne to them. By faith we understand that the worlds have been framed by the word of God, so that what is seen hath not been made out of things which appear.

Heb. 11:1-3

Being therefore justified by faith, we have peace with God through our Lord Jesus Christ; through whom also we have had our access by faith into this grace wherein we stand; and we rejoice in hope of the glory of God. And not only so, but we also rejoice in our tribulations: knowing that tribulation worketh steadfastness; and steadfastness, approvedness; and approvedness, hope: and hope putteth not to shame; because the love of God hath been shed abroad in our hearts through the Holy Spirit which was given unto us.

Romans 5:1-5

LISTENING TO GOD
Grade Four

LISTENING TO GOD

Grade Four

By
MABEL NATALIE ERICKSEN

Illustrated by
Stryker Ingerman

This volume is one in a series of graded Sunday school textbooks issued by the Board of Elementary Christian Education, Dr. Jacob Tanner, editor-in-chief

Published by AUGSBURG PUBLISHING HOUSE, *Minneapolis*

LISTENING TO GOD
Copyright, 1938
Augsburg Publishing House

Manufactured in the United States of America

A LETTER TO THE CHILDREN

Dear children:

Do you want to know the men and women that God called to work in His kingdom on earth? It takes a large book to tell about all of them. We have such a book. It is the Bible. When you are older you will read about them all from this Book. This little lesson book that you now hold in your hand tells about some of them and about Jesus. The whole world loves and knows Him. Every child is better off and millions of people are happier because He came to earth as man for a while.

As you read about these men and women they will interest you more and more. You will not find in all the stories ever told any more interesting people than these. Most of them remained true to God and His work. A few fell away because they listened to men and followed their own evil ways instead of listening to God. Others that had a chance to work in His kingdom worked against Him, but we know they worked harm to themselves because no one can harm God.

Is it not wonderful to know that Jesus places children in His kingdom as workers as well as He does grown people? Jesus said, "Suffer the little children, and forbid them not, to come unto me: for to such belongeth the kingdom of heaven" (Matt. 19:14). In the next verse, 15, it says, "And he laid his hands on them and departed thence." Clearly then we see that Jesus blessed little children for work in His kingdom. The best way to do this work is as Jesus did: read your Bibles, go to Sunday school and church, and the rest will come as God has promised. Let us begin now. Find Matthew 19 and let us read verses 14 and 15. Turn to Chapter 1 which tells you more about what we have just said. With Jesus' blessing upon us we begin in His name.

Your friend and author of Book IV,
MABEL NATALIE ERICKSEN.

Table of Contents

CHAPTER	TITLE	PAGE
	Luther's Small Catechism	9
1.	The Word of God	25

PART I—THE TEN COMMANDMENTS

2.	*The First Commandment*—God Calls Isaiah	28
3.	*The Second Commandment*—Job	31
4.	*The Third Commandment*—The Day of Rest in the Wilderness	34
5.	*The Fourth Commandment*—Jesus, the Obedient Boy	37
6.	*The Fifth Commandment*—Herod, the Wicked Ruler	40
7.	*The Sixth Commandment*—The Woman of Samaria	43
8.	*The Seventh Commandment*—Samuel, the Honest Steward	46
9.	*The Eighth Commandment*—False Witness Against Naboth	49
10.	*The Ninth and Tenth Commandments*—Gehazi, or the Sin of Covetousness	52
11.	*God's Declaration*—Punishments and Blessings	55

PART II—THE CREED

12.	*The First Article*—Zacharias	61
13.	*The First Article*—God Blesses Abraham	64
14.	*The First Article*—Peter's Escape from Prison	67
15.	*The Second Article*—The First Christmas	70
16.	*The Second Article*—The Man Born Blind	73
17.	*The Second Article*—The Suffering and Death of Jesus	76
18.	*The Second Article*—The Risen Christ	79
19.	*The Third Article*—Pentecost	83
20.	*The Third Article*—A Sinner Saved	86
21.	*The Third Article*—Jesus Raises Jairus' Daughter	89

PART III—THE LORD'S PRAYER

22. *The Introduction*—Jesus in Prayer 92
23. *The First Petition*—Paul Fights for the Pure Gospel 96
24. *The Second Petition*—Paul and the Philippians 99
25. *The Third Petition*—Paul, the Sufferer for Christ 102
26. *The Fourth Petition*—Paul the Missionary 105
27. *The Fifth Petition*—Stephen, the First Martyr 108
28. *The Sixth Petition*—Judas Betrays Jesus 112
29. *The Seventh Petition*—Saul Pursues David 115
30. *The Conclusion*—God Answers Moses 118

PART IV—THE SACRAMENT OF BAPTISM

31. *Baptism I and II*—Jesus Institutes Baptism 121
32. *Baptism III*—Cornelius Is Baptized 125
33. *Baptism IV*—Paul Fighting the Good Fight 128
34. *Confession*—The Lost Son 131

PART V—THE SACRAMENT OF THE ALTAR

35. *The Lord's Supper I and II*—Jesus Institutes the Lord's Supper ... 134
36. *The Lord's Supper III and IV*—Early Christians at the Lord's Supper 138
    Hymns 141

Luther's Small Catechism

Part I
The Ten Commandments

THE INTRODUCTION
I am the Lord thy God.

THE FIRST COMMANDMENT
Thou shalt have no other gods before Me.

What does this mean?

We should fear, love, and trust in God above all things.

THE SECOND COMMANDMENT
Thou shalt not take the name of the Lord thy God in vain; for the Lord will not hold him guiltless that taketh His name in vain.

What does this mean?

We should fear and love God so that we do not curse, swear, conjure, lie, or deceive, by His name, but call upon Him in every time of need, and worship Him with prayer, praise, and thanksgiving.

THE THIRD COMMANDMENT
Remember the Sabbath day, to keep it holy.

What does this mean?

We should fear and love God so that we do not despise His Word and the preaching of the same, but deem it holy, and gladly hear and learn it.

THE FOURTH COMMANDMENT
Honor thy father and thy mother, that thy days may be long upon the land which the Lord thy God giveth thee

What does this mean?

We should fear and love God so that we do not despise our parents and superiors, nor provoke them to anger, but honor, serve, obey, love, and esteem them.

THE FIFTH COMMANDMENT

Thou shalt not kill.

What does this mean?

We should fear and love God so that we do our neighbor no bodily harm nor cause him any suffering, but help and befriend him in every need.

THE SIXTH COMMANDMENT

Thou shalt not commit adultery.

What does this mean?

We should fear and love God so that we lead a chaste and pure life in word and deed, and that husband and wife love and honor each other.

THE SEVENTH COMMANDMENT

Thou shalt not steal.

What does this mean?

We should fear and love God so that we do not rob our neighbor of his money or property, nor bring them into our possession by unfair dealing or fraud, but help him to improve and protect his property and living.

THE EIGHTH COMMANDMENT

Thou shalt not bear false witness against thy neighbor.

What does this mean?

We should fear and love God so that we do not deceitfully belie, betray, backbite, nor slander our neighbor, but apologize for him, speak well of him, and put the most charitable construction on all that he does.

THE NINTH COMMANDMENT

Thou shalt not covet thy neighbor's house.

What does this mean?

We should fear and love God so that we do not seek by craftiness to gain possession of our neighbor's inheritance or home nor obtain them under pretense of a legal right, but assist and serve him in keeping the same.

THE TENTH COMMANDMENT

Thou shalt not covet thy neighbor's wife, nor his manservant, nor his maidservant, nor his cattle, nor anything that is thy neighbor's.

What does this mean?

We should fear and love God so that we do not estrange or entice away our neighbor's wife, servants, or cattle, but seek to have them remain and discharge their duty to him.

THE CONCLUSION

What does God declare concerning all these commandments?

He says: I the Lord thy God am a jealous God, visiting the iniquity of the fathers upon the children unto the third and fourth generation of them that hate Me; and showing mercy unto thousands of them that love Me and keep My commandments.

What does this mean?

God threatens to punish all who transgress these commandments. We should, therefore, fear His wrath, and in no wise disobey them. But He promises grace and every blessing to all who keep them. We should, therefore, love Him, trust in Him, and gladly keep His commandments.

Part II
The Creed

THE FIRST ARTICLE
OF CREATION

I believe in God the Father almighty, Maker of heaven and earth.

What does this mean?

I believe that God has created me and all that exists; that He has given and still preserves to me my body and soul, my eyes and ears, and all my members, my reason and all the powers of my soul, together with food and raiment, home and family, and all my property; that He daily provides abundantly for all the needs of my life, protects me from all danger, and guards and keeps me from all evil; and that He does this purely out of fatherly and divine goodness and mercy, without any merit or worthiness in me; for all of which I am in duty bound to thank, praise, serve, and obey Him. This is most certainly true.

THE SECOND ARTICLE
OF REDEMPTION

And in Jesus Christ His only Son, our Lord; who was conceived by the Holy Spirit, born of the Virgin Mary; suffered under Pontius Pilate, was crucified, dead, and buried; He descended into hell; the third day He rose again from the dead; He ascended into heaven, and sitteth on the right hand of God the Father almighty; from thence He shall come to judge the quick and the dead.

What does this mean?

I believe that Jesus Christ, true God, begotten of the Father from eternity, and also true Man, born of the Virgin Mary, is my Lord; who has redeemed me, a lost and condemned creature, bought me and freed me from all sins, from death, and from the power of the devil; not with silver and gold, but with His holy and precious blood, and with His innocent sufferings and death;

in order that I might be His own, live under Him in His kingdom, and serve Him in everlasting righteousness, innocence, and blessedness; even as He is risen from the dead, and lives and reigns to all eternity. This is most certainly true.

THE THIRD ARTICLE
OF SANCTIFICATION

I believe in the Holy Spirit; the holy Christian Church, the Communion of Saints; the forgiveness of sins; the resurrection of the body and the life everlasting.

What does this mean?

I believe that I cannot by my own reason or strength believe in Jesus Christ my Lord, or come to Him; but the Holy Spirit has called me through the Gospel, enlightened me with His gifts, and sanctified and preserved me in the true faith; in like manner as He calls, gathers, enlightens and sanctifies the whole Christian Church on earth, and preserves it in union with Jesus Christ in the one true faith; in which Christian Church He daily forgives abundantly all my sins, and the sins of all believers, and at the last day will raise up me and all the dead, and will grant everlasting life to me and to all who believe in Christ. This is most certainly true.

Part III
The Lord's Prayer

THE INTRODUCTION

Our Father, who art in heaven.

What does this mean?

God thereby tenderly encourages us to believe that He is truly our Father, and that we are truly His children, so that we may boldly and confidently come to Him in prayer, even as beloved children come to their dear father.

THE FIRST PETITION

Hallowed be Thy name.

What does this mean?

God's name is indeed holy in itself; but we pray in this petition that it may be hallowed also among us.

How is this done?

When the Word of God is taught in its truth and purity and we, as God's children, lead holy lives, in accordance with it. This grant us, dear Father in heaven! But whoever teaches and lives otherwise than God's Word teaches, profanes the name of God among us. From this preserve us, heavenly Father!

THE SECOND PETITION

Thy kingdom come.

What does this mean?

The kingdom of God comes indeed of itself, without our prayer; but we pray in this petition that it may come also to us.

How is this done?

When our heavenly Father gives us His Holy Spirit, so that by His grace we believe His holy Word, and live a godly life here on earth, and in heaven for ever.

THE THIRD PETITION

Thy will be done on earth, as it is in heaven.

What does this mean?

The good and gracious will of God is done indeed without our prayer; but we pray in this petition that it may be done also among us.

How is this done?

When God destroys and brings to naught every evil counsel and purpose of the devil, the world, and our own flesh, which would hinder us from hallowing His name, and prevent the coming of His kingdom; and when He strengthens us and keeps us steadfast in His Word and in faith, even unto our end. This is His good and gracious will.

THE FOURTH PETITION

Give us this day our daily bread.

What does this mean?

God indeed gives daily bread to all men, even to the wicked, without our prayer; but we pray in this petition that He would lead us to acknowledge our daily bread as His gift, and to receive it with thanksgiving.

What is meant by daily bread?

Everything that is required to satisfy our bodily needs; such as food and raiment, house and home, fields and flocks, money and goods; pious parents, children, and servants; godly and faithful rulers, good government; seasonable weather, peace and health; order and honor; true friends, good neighbors, and the like.

THE FIFTH PETITION

And forgive us our trespasses, as we forgive those who trespass against us.

What does this mean?

We pray in this petition that our heavenly Father would not regard our sins nor because of them deny our prayers; for we neither merit nor are worthy of those things for which we pray;

but that He would grant us all things through grace, even though we sin daily, and deserve nothing but punishment. And certainly we, on our part, will heartily forgive, and gladly do good to those who may sin against us.

THE SIXTH PETITION

And lead us not into temptation.

What does this mean?

God indeed tempts no one to sin; but we pray in this petition that God would so guard and preserve us, that the devil, the world, and our own flesh may not deceive us, nor lead us into error and unbelief, despair, and other great and shameful sins; but that, when so tempted, we may finally prevail and gain the victory.

THE SEVENTH PETITION

But deliver us from evil.

What does this mean?

We pray in this petition, as in a summary, that our heavenly Father would deliver us from all manner of evil, whether it affect body or soul, property or reputation, and at last, when the hour of death shall come, grant us a blessed end, and graciously take us from this world of sorrow to Himself in heaven.

THE CONCLUSION

For Thine is the kingdom, and the power, and the glory, for ever and ever. Amen.

What does the word "Amen" mean?

It means that I should be assured that such petitions are acceptable to our heavenly Father, and are heard by Him; for He Himself has commanded us to pray in this manner, and has promised to hear us. Amen, Amen, that is, Yea, yea, it shall be so.

Part IV
The Sacrament of Baptism

I
WHAT IS BAPTISM?

Baptism is not simply water, but it is the water used according to God's command and connected with God's word.

What is this word of God?

It is the word of our Lord Jesus Christ, as recorded in the last chapter of Matthew: "Go ye therefore, and make disciples of all the nations, baptizing them into the name of the Father and of the Son and of the Holy Spirit."

II
WHAT GIFTS OR BENEFITS DOES BAPTISM BESTOW?

It works forgiveness of sins, delivers from death and the devil, and gives everlasting salvation to all who believe, as the word and promise of God declares.

What is this word and promise of God?

It is the word of our Lord Jesus Christ, as recorded in the last chapter of Mark: "He that believeth and is baptized shall be saved; but he that disbelieveth shall be condemned."

III
HOW CAN WATER DO SUCH GREAT THINGS?

It is not the water, indeed, that does such great things, but the word of God, connected with the water, and our faith which relies on that word of God. For without the word of God, it is simply water and no baptism. But when connected with the word of God, it is a baptism, that is, a gracious water of life and a washing of regeneration in the Holy Spirit, as St. Paul says to Titus, in the third chapter: "According to His mercy He saved us, through the washing of regeneration and renewing of the Holy Spirit, which He poured out upon us richly, through Jesus Christ our Savior; that, being justified by His grace, we might be made heirs according to the hope of eternal life. This is a faithful saying."

IV

WHAT DOES SUCH BAPTIZING WITH WATER SIGNIFY?

It signifies that the old Adam in us, together with all sins and evil lusts, should be drowned by daily sorrow and repentance, and be put to death; and that the new man should daily come forth and rise, to live before God in righteousness and holiness for ever.

Where is it so written?

St. Paul, in the sixth chapter of the Epistle to the Romans, says: "We were buried therefore with Him through baptism into death: that like as Christ was raised from the dead through the glory of the Father, so we also might walk in newness of life."

OF CONFESSION

What is Confession?

Confession consists of two parts: the one is that we confess our sins; the other, that we receive absolution or forgiveness from the pastor as from God Himself, in no wise doubting, but firmly believing, that our sins are thereby forgiven before God in heaven.

What sins should we confess?

Before God we should acknowledge ourselves guilty of all manner of sins, even of those of which we are not aware, as we do in the Lord's Prayer. To the pastor we should confess only those sins which we know and feel in our hearts.

What are such sins?

Here examine yourself in the light of the Ten Commandments, whether as father or mother, son or daughter, master or servant, you have been disobedient, unfaithful, slothful, illtempered, unchaste, or quarrelsome, or whether you have injured any one by word or deed, stolen, neglected, or wasted aught, or done any other evil.

Part V
The Sacrament of the Altar

I

WHAT IS THE SACRAMENT OF THE ALTAR?

It is the true Body and Blood of our Lord Jesus Christ, under the bread and wine, given unto us Christians to eat and to drink, as it was instituted by Christ Himself.

Where is it so written?

The holy Evangelists, Matthew, Mark, and Luke, together with St. Paul, write thus:

"Our Lord Jesus Christ, in the night in which He was betrayed, took bread; and when He had given thanks, He brake it and gave it to His disciples, saying, Take, eat; this is My Body, which is given for you; this do in remembrance of Me.

"After the same manner, also, He took the cup, when He had supped, and when He had given thanks, He gave it to them, saying, Drink ye all of it; this cup is the new testament in My Blood, which is shed for you, and for many, for the remission of sins; this do, as oft as ye drink it, in remembrance of Me."

II

WHAT IS THE BENEFIT OF SUCH EATING AND DRINKING?

It is pointed out in these words: "Given and shed for you for the remission of sins." Through these words the remission of sins, life and salvation are given unto us in the Sacrament; for where there is remission of sins, there is also life and salvation.

III

HOW CAN THE BODILY EATING AND DRINKING PRODUCE SUCH GREAT BENEFITS?

The eating and drinking, indeed, do not produce them, but the words: "Given and shed for you for the remission of sins." For besides the bodily eating and drinking, these words are the chief thing in the Sacrament; and he who believes them has what they say and declare, namely, the remission of sins.

IV
WHO, THEN, RECEIVES THE SACRAMENT WORTHILY?

Fasting and bodily preparation are indeed a good outward discipline, but he is truly worthy and well prepared who believes these words: "Given and shed for you for the remission of sins." But he who does not believe these words or who doubts them is unworthy and unprepared; for the words: "For you," require truly believing hearts.

Chapter 1

The Word of God

ONE day when Jesus sat by the seaside a crowd of people gathered about Him. He stepped into a boat and spoke to the people on the shore. He talked about the Word of God and what use some people make of it. He told them the story of the Sower.

A sower went out to sow. As he sowed some seed fell by the wayside. The birds came and ate it. Some of the seed fell on rocky ground. The sun quickly scorched the growing plants because they had no soil to grow in. Some of the seed fell among thorns and the thorns choked it.

But some fell upon good ground and bore fruit, some a hundred-fold, some sixty-fold, and some thirty-fold.

In this story Jesus points out that it is our hearts that make it easy or hard for the seed to grow. The seed God sows is His Word, through which He brings salvation to man. In the Old Testament He gave His Word to those who accepted it and used it. He gave it to Adam, Noah, Abraham, and others. At Mount Sinai He gave it to Moses for the nation of Israel. Then He told Moses, Isaiah, Micah, and other prophets to write it down for people not yet born into the world.

In the New Testament Jesus taught the Word of God to people in a way it had never been taught before. God led Matthew, John, Paul, and other disciples of Christ to write the New Testament.

A Sower Went Out to Sow

The Holy Spirit, working through those who believe in Jesus Christ, is always at work sowing the Word of God. God wants all people to hear His Word. If we hear it, believe it, and obey it, the Word of God will grow and bear good fruit.

There are many things that come into the heart and work against His Word. The Word of God can not grow in an untruthful, bitter, and evil heart. People who receive the Word and use it grow good fruit. They spread the Word because they love God and want to bring souls to Him.

In our Catechism, too, we have the Word of God. It gives the teachings of the Bible. It was written by a man whose heart loved the Word and bore a hundred-fold harvest. This man was Martin Luther.

When Luther became a pastor in Germany he found that many people did not know the Word of God. Very few had seen the Bible. Still fewer could read it because it was written in Latin. Luther translated it into the language of the people. To help them understand its teachings he wrote the Catechism.

Through the use of the Catechism children learn to understand the truth taught in the Bible. Our hearts should be places where the Word of God can take root, grow, and bear fruit for His kingdom. (This story is based on Matthew 13:1-23.)

Some Seed Fell Among Thorns

Luther Translating the Bible

LESSON TEXT

He that hath ears, let him hear. Matthew 13:9.

HYMN (See page 141)

PRAYER

My God and Father, I thank Thee for Thy Word. Speak to me that I may know Thee and serve Thee. Amen.

BIBLE STUDY

1. Which is the first book in the New Testament?
2. Can you name the next three books?
3. Look up all these four books in your Bible.
4. What are these four books called?
5. Find Matthew 13:1-23 and read it.
6. When does the Word of God bear good fruit? (Matthew 13:23.)

QUESTIONS

1. How did the Word of God come to earth?
2. Where do we read the Word? Who wrote it?
3. What does Christ say about listening to the Word?
4. Why did Jesus tell the parable of the Sower?
5. Who wrote our Catechism? Why did he write it?
6. In what way is the Catechism like the Bible?
7. How does the Catechism help us?

Chapter 2

THE INTRODUCTION

I am the Lord thy God.

THE FIRST COMMANDMENT

Thou shalt have no other gods before Me.

QUESTION: What does this mean?

ANSWER: We should fear, love, and trust in God above all things.

God Calls Isaiah

GOD needed a man to do some very hard and important work for Him among His people. They were worshipping idols. Their nation was in danger of being wiped off the earth. God had sent them prophets to warn them to return to the Lord, but they had not listened. Now a prophet was needed to tell them what was going to happen to them for leaving God.

They were to be carried away as prisoners into a strange land. Enemies were to burn their cities, even Jerusalem and its beautiful temple. Only one thing could save them. God would send His Son, Jesus Christ, into the world to suffer and die on the cross for them. They must understand this in order to make themselves ready for His coming. They must turn away from idols. They must teach their children the way back to God so that their nation might live.

It would be hard to make them understand this. They were hardened in sin and would refuse to listen to any teacher. Isaiah was the right man for this hard work, but he needed to understand God's holiness more fully. He also needed to know that God planned to send Jesus Christ to earth to die for their sins.

So God gave Isaiah a vision. He saw God on His throne and around it angels singing praises to Him. The angels found no words strong enough to tell their reverence for Him, so they sang over and over again, "Holy, holy, holy." They sang until the sound shook the groundwork of the temple.

Such glory and majesty Isaiah had never dreamed of. He was frightened, and dismayed. He felt himself unworthy to stand

Isaiah and the Angel

in the presence of the holy God. He could not join in that song, nor could the people of Israel. They were sinners and their lips were unclean in the sight of the holy, righteous God.

In this way God made Isaiah see how sin had parted them from God. Isaiah confessed his uncleanness. He cried out, *Woe is me.* Then an angel flew to the altar with a tong. He took a live coal from the altar and touched it to Isaiah's lips. The angel said, *Lo, this has touched thy lips; and thine iniquity is taken away, and thy sin forgiven.*

This meant that Jesus would bring forgiveness for the sins of the world.

Isaiah understood this. He also understood that God really forgives our sin and makes us fear, love, and trust Him when we confess our sin. Isaiah felt happy. He wished he could tell the people how God would save them, if they would confess their sin. When God asked, Who will go for us? Isaiah answered in greatest awe, reverence, and joy, *Here am I; send me.*

Isaiah went out to tell the people what was to happen to them. He also told them about the way back to God through Jesus Christ. (This story is based on Isaiah 6:1-8.)

LESSON TEXT

Holy, holy, holy is the Lord of hosts. Isaiah 6:3.

HYMN (See page 141)

PRAYER

Create in me a clean heart, O God; and renew a right spirit within me. Amen.

BIBLE STUDY

1. Name the first four books in the New Testament.
2. Find the Book of Isaiah. Is it in the Old Testament or in the New?
3. Look up the four books that come after Isaiah. Name them.
4. The four men who wrote these books are called the Major Prophets.
5. Find Isaiah 6:1-8. Read it.

QUESTIONS

1. Why did God give Isaiah this vision?
2. What kind of man was Isaiah? Why would his work be hard?
3. What two things did Isaiah learn from the vision?
4. What did the angels sing? Why?
5. How did the angels show their reverence for God? Is. 6:1-6.
6. Why did the angel touch Isaiah's lips with coal?
7. Why was he now ready to do God's work?
8. How did he offer himself to God?

Chapter 3

THE SECOND COMMANDMENT

Thou shalt not take the name of the Lord thy God in vain; for the Lord will not hold him guiltless that taketh His name in vain.

QUESTION: What does this mean?

ANSWER: We should fear and love God so that we do not curse, swear, conjure, lie, or deceive, by His name, but call upon Him in every time of need, and worship Him with prayer, praise, and thanksgiving.

Job

JOB lived in the land of Uz. He was a good man who feared and loved God. He had seven son and three daughters. He owned seven thousand sheep and three thousand camels and hundreds of asses and yokes of oxen. And he had many servants to take care of all his property.

When his children grew up and married, Job kept on praying for them. When they had been feasting he got up early and offered sacrifices to the Lord for all of them. He said, *It may be that my sons have sinned, and renounced God in their hearts.*

Naturally, Job was highly respected and honored.

Satan did not like Job. He had not been able to lead him away from God. One day he said to God that it was easy for Job to fear God and keep from evil. God had given him more than he needed. *But,* said Satan, *put forth Thy hand now, and touch all that he hath, and he will renounce Thee to Thy face.*

So God gave Satan permission to test Job's faith and love.

One day one of the servants came running to Job and said: *The oxen were plowing, and the asses feeding beside them; and the Sabeans fell upon them and took them away: yea, they have slain the servants with the edge of the sword; and I only am escaped alone to tell thee.*

He was not through speaking before another servant rushed up to Job. He told that lightning had killed the sheep and the servants that took care of them.

He had not finished before another came with sad news. The Chaldeans had taken all the camels and killed their keepers.

And then came the hardest blow. Another servant brought the

news that a storm had destroyed the house where his children were feasting and killed them all.

Then Job arose, and rent his robe, and shaved his head, and fell down upon the ground and worshipped; and he said, ... *The Lord gave, and the Lord hath taken away; blessed be the name of the Lord.* In all this Job did not sin.

God let new trials come upon Job. Boils covered him from head to foot. The itching pain was so terrible that he kept scratching himself with a potsherd. His wife lost her faith in God and said to him, *Renounce God, and die.* But Job answered, *What? Shall we receive good at the hand of God, and shall we not receive evil?* In all this Job did not sin.

When three of Job's friends in other parts of the land heard what had happened they came to comfort him. They were shocked at what they saw. They thought that he surely must have sinned greatly since he had to suffer so much. And they

Job's Servants Bring Bad News

sat there seven days and seven nights without saying a word.

Job felt that they blamed him for his trouble. He thought this was unjust. It made him bitter and he cursed the day he was born. He accused God of being unjust to him.

At last God spoke to Job in a storm. He made him see that he was not able to understand God's wisdom and plans. Job admitted he had sinned by accusing God of being unjust, and said: *I abhor myself, and repent in dust and ashes.*

Then God again blessed Job both with children and property. (This story is based on Job 1; 2; 38; 42.)

LESSON TEXT

The Lord gave, and the Lord hath taken away; blessed be the name of the Lord. Job 1:21.

HYMN (See page 141)

Job Prays

PRAYER

Our Father in heaven, Hallowed be Thy name. Amen.

BIBLE STUDY

1. Name the four Major Prophets.
2. Find the Book of Job.
3. Look up the four books that come after Job. Name them.
4. Find Job 19:25-27. Of whom does Job speak here?

QUESTIONS

1. What is the Second Commandment? What does it mean?
2. What is the most common way of taking God's name in vain?
3. What did Job say when he had lost his children?
4. What did Job's wife tell him to do? What did he answer?
5. Why did God let such trouble come upon Job?
6. How did Job sin?
7. What did God teach him in the storm?
8. What did Job then say?

Chapter 4

THE THIRD COMMANDMENT

Remember the Sabbath day, to keep it holy.

QUESTION: What does this mean?

ANSWER: We should fear and love God so that we do not despise His Word and the preaching of the same, but deem it holy, and gladly hear and learn it.

The Day of Rest in the Wilderness

GOD'S people have always had a weekly day of rest. It is called the Sabbath Day, which means the Rest Day. God gave us the day for two reasons. We should rest from our labor and gather strength for the work of the new week. We should also use this day for coming together for public worship. The Day of Rest is kept holy when we use it as God wants us to use it.

Many were the ways that God used to impress upon the people of Israel that they should keep the Sabbath holy. Today we shall learn how God taught them that they should work six days for their food, but on the Sabbath Day they should rest.

When the people of Israel left Egypt, they traveled through a wilderness where they could find no food. The people complained bitterly against Moses and Aaron, his brother. They blamed Moses for every hardship, forgetting that they had been very glad to leave the land of slavery. Now they wished they were back in Egypt where, they claimed, they had more than enough to eat. Listen to this unjust accusation against Moses and his brother: *Ye have brought us forth into this wilderness, to kill this whole assembly with hunger.*

As was his custom, Moses brought the trouble to God. And God spoke to Moses, *I have heard the murmurings of the children of Israel: speak unto them, saying, At even ye shall eat flesh, and in the morning ye shall be filled with bread; and ye shall know that I am the Lord your God.*

In the evening large flocks of quail covered the camp and in the morning small round white things, like small seed kernels,

Gathering Manna

were upon the ground. When the people saw it, they said, "Manna? Manna?" That is, "What is it? What is it?" Moses said unto them, *It is the bread which the Lord hath given you to eat.*

Moses told the people that on each morning they should gather as much as they needed for food that day. On the sixth day he told them that they should gather enough for two days, for on the Sabbath Day there would be no manna on the ground. *Tomorrow is solemn rest, a holy Sabbath unto the Lord.*

As usual, many paid no attention to what Moses said. Either they did not gather enough manna on the sixth day or they did not prepare it so it would keep for two days. So on the Sabbath morning they went out to gather manna for the day, but they found none. And the Lord said to Moses:

How long refuse ye to keep My commandments and My laws? See, for that the Lord hath given you the Sabbath, therefore He giveth you on the sixth day the bread of two days; abide ye every man in his place, let no man go out of his place on the seventh day.

So the people rested on the seventh day. (This story is based on Exodus 16:1-30.)

LESSON TEXT

Remember the sabbath day to keep it holy. Exodus 20:8.

HYMN (See page 141)

PRAYER

Dear Lord, we thank Thee for Sunday, our day of rest. Forgive us when we misuse it and help us to keep it holy. Amen.

BIBLE STUDY

1. Name the first four books in the New Testament.
2. Name the Major Prophets.
3. Name the poetical books of the Old Testament.
4. Find the second book in the Bible. What is its name?
5. What is the name of the first book of the Bible?
6. Of the third, fourth, and fifth books?
7. Find Exodus 20:8. Read it.

QUESTIONS

1. What is the Third Commandment? What does it mean?
2. In what ways do we keep the day of rest holy? (See "Answer" under Commandment.)
3. How many days a week should we work for our living?
4. Why did the people of Israel complain against Moses and Aaron?
5. How were they unfair in their accusation?
6. What does the word manna mean?
7. How much should they gather each day?
8. Why should they on the sixth day gather for two days?
9. Why did not all obey?
10. What did God say to Moses?
11. To whom did Moses bring the words of God?
12. What was the result?

On the Way to the Synagogue

Chapter 5

THE FOURTH COMMANDMENT

Honor thy father and thy mother, that thy days may be long upon the land which the Lord thy God giveth thee.

QUESTION: What does this mean?

ANSWER: We should fear and love God so that we do not despise our parents and superiors, nor provoke them to anger, but honor, serve, obey, love, and esteem them.

Jesus, the Obedient Boy

AFTER a short stay in Egypt, Joseph and Mary returned to their own home town of Nazareth. Here our Savior spent most of His life on earth. The Bible tells us that as He grew *Jesus advanced in wisdom and stature, and in favor with God and man.*

Jesus enjoyed all that made Nazareth beautiful: birds, bees, flowers, trees, hills, vineyards, fields. No doubt He was much interested in the lively trade brought in by the caravans. His time and mind were filled with work, play, home, friends, school, and His heavenly Father.

His home training and teaching taught Him to know God, His Father. The Bible says, He was *filled with wisdom: and the*

Praising God in Song

grace of God was upon Him. From Mary He learned the Ten Commandments, the Psalms, and God's promise to send Israel a Messiah who was to save the people from their sins. He listened eagerly to the stories about Abraham, Moses, Joseph, David, Ruth, Daniel, and others of God's people, many of them His own ancestors. He held Mary's hand firmly when they went to the synagogue. He sat very still listening to every word.

Because He was without sin He was not afraid of God but early learned to love Him. He wanted to do His Father's will. How happy He must have been when for the first time He repeated without help the Jewish Confession of Faith which reads: *Hear, O Israel: the Lord our God is one Lord: and thou shalt love the Lord thy God with all thy heart, and with all thy soul, and with all thy might.* And this the boy Jesus did.

In the synagogue school the Old Testament was His only textbook until He was twelve years old. What a light must have flashed from His fearless eyes as He read the lessons He loved! How clear and reverent His voice must have been! How eagerly He must have searched His Book for God's truth and will, not just to please His teachers, but to learn what His heavenly Father wanted Him to do.

And He waxed strong as He grew. What boy or girl who grows strong and healthy does not like to play? Surely Jesus played and enjoyed it as much as any boy does today. If He ever was tempted to disobey, as you and I are, when His parents called Him from play, He asked God to give Him willing obedience. Even though He was strong He was kind and fair to His playmates. How else could He have grown in favor with God and man?

And He was dutiful toward His parents as He grew from perfect boyhood into perfect manhood. Luke says, *He was subject unto them.* He helped His father and mother with His little hands and His willing obedience. (This story is based on Luke 2:40, 51, 52.)

LESSON TEXT

Children, obey your parents in the Lord: for this is right. Ephesians 6:1.

HYMN (See page 141)

PRAYER

Teach me to love, honor, and obey my parents and my superiors and to love Thee, my Lord and Savior. Amen.

BIBLE STUDY

1. Name the four Gospels in the order they follow each other in the Bible.
2. The third Gospel was written by a doctor. What was his name? He was one of Paul's helpers.
3. Find Luke 2:40, 51, 52. Read these verses.
4. Find Deuteronomy 6:4-5. Read it.
5. How did Jesus abide in His Father's love? Find the answer in John 5:30 and 15:10.
6. Find Hebrews 13:17. Read it.
7. Find Acts 5:29. Read it.
8. Find Ephesians 6:1. Read it.

QUESTIONS

1. How did Jesus keep the Fourth Commandment?
2. What does it mean to honor your parents?
3. How did Jesus treat other children?
4. Why did people like the boy Jesus?
5. How do we know Jesus loved nature? (His parables are about nature.)
6. How does Jesus' school compare with yours?
7. Why should we obey our parents? (Lesson Text.)
8. Whom besides your parents should you obey? (Hebrews 13:17.)
9. Should you obey if they ask you to do wrong? (Acts 5:29.)
10. How can we learn obedience?

Helpful Obedience

The Wise Men and the Star

Chapter 6

THE FIFTH COMMANDMENT

Thou shalt not kill.

QUESTION: What does this mean?

ANSWER: We should fear and love God so that we do our neighbor no bodily harm nor cause him any suffering, but help and befriend him in every need.

Herod, the Wicked Ruler

HEROD was ruler of Judea when Jesus was born. He was known all over the land for his selfishness and cruelty. He knew how people feared and hated him. He tried to win their favor by making the temple at Jerusalem beautiful. He wanted to make sure that there would be sorrow in the land when he died. When on his deathbed, he ordered that seventy of the leading men be put into prison and killed as soon as he died.

We are glad that these men were not put to death. Into the land of such a ruler our Savior was born!

Herod was afraid when he heard that the King of the Jews was born. He called the scribes and the chief priests to him and asked them where this king was to be born. They reminded him of the prophecy in Micah 5:2, which says that Christ was to be born in Bethlehem, only a few miles from Jerusalem. Herod planned to do something before this new-born King of the Jews should take the kingdom from him.

He called the Wise Men and asked them when they had seen His star. When they had told him he sent them to Bethlehem. He ordered them to come back to him when they had found Christ so that he, too, might go to worship. What he planned to do was to send soldiers to kill the baby. But the Wise Men, after they found the Christ Child, were warned by an angel to go home by another road.

How angry Herod was when they did not return to him! But murder did not leave his mind. To be sure that Jesus would be killed, he ordered all boy babies two years old and under in Bethlehem to be put to death. The awful sorrow of the fathers and mothers did not touch his heart. How could it? He had killed his wife and three of his sons for the same reason he was killing these children—to keep his throne for himself. But he did not succeed in destroying Jesus!

God sent an angel to tell Joseph to flee into Egypt with the baby and its mother. It is truly wonderful how God takes care of His own. Perhaps the gold, frankincense, and myrrh that the Wise Men had given Jesus paid the expenses of the trip.

After some time the angel told them that Herod was dead and that it was safe for them to return home. Then the holy family went back into the land of Israel and lived in Nazareth of Galilee. (This story is based on Matthew 2:1-16).

Herod and the Wise Men

LESSON TEXT

The Lord will keep thee from all evil. Psalm 121:7.

HYMN (See page 141)

PRAYER

Make me to walk in Thy commands;
'Tis a delightful road:
Nor let my head or heart or hands
Offend against my God. Amen.

BIBLE STUDY

1. Name the poetical books of the Bible.
2. What book comes before the poetical books? What comes after?
3. Find Psalm 121:7. Read it.
4. Find Micah 5:2. Of whom is this said?
5. Look up Matthew 2:5-6. What do these verses say of Micah 5:2?
6. Micah is one of the Minor Prophets. There are twelve Minor Prophets.
7. Find Matthew 2:1-16. Read it.

QUESTIONS

1. Who was Herod? Why was he so cruel?
2. What is the Lesson Text? Whom did God keep safe in our story? Why?
3. Why did Herod want to find Jesus? In what two ways did he try to find him? Why did he fail each time?
4. Why was not Herod sorry for the mothers and fathers whose children he killed?
5. Find two places that prove that Herod lied to the Wise Men. What commandment did he break?

Joseph and Mary Flee to Egypt

Chapter 7

THE SIXTH COMMANDMENT

Thou shalt not commit adultery.

QUESTION: What does this mean?

ANSWER: We should fear and love God so that we lead a chaste and pure life in word and deed, and that husband and wife love and honor each other.

The Woman of Samaria

ON His way from Judea to Galilee, Jesus rested beside Jacob's well in Samaria. The disciples had gone into the city of Sychar to buy food, for it was near noon. Jesus found it good to rest alone in the beautiful place that Jacob had given his son, Joseph. Perhaps Jesus was thinking about this Old Testament hero.

Perhaps, too, He was thinking about the Samaritans in whose land He was. Some of them were kinder to each other and to Him than were His own people, the Jews. But the Jews looked down on the Samaritans and would have nothing to do with them.

Jesus was not to be alone long. A woman of Samaria came to the well to draw water. She was not a good woman and Jesus knew it. When He asked her for a drink, she was surprised that He, a Jew, should ask her for a drink of water, and she told Him so. Jesus told her that if she but knew Him, she would ask Him for a drink and He would give her living water.

She did not understand what He meant by living water; but she knew about the promised Messiah. She asked Jesus how He could get water from the deep well, when He had nothing to draw it with. Again He tried to make her see what He meant. He told her that whoever drank of the living water would never thirst again. Then she asked Him to give her that water so she would not have to come back to the well for water every day.

Jesus said, *Go, call thy husband, and come hither.* She answered, *I have no husband.*

She began to understand that Jesus was not an ordinary man. He said, *Thou saidst well, I have no husband: for thou hast had*

Jesus at the Well

five husbands; and he whom thou now hast is not thy husband: this hast thou said truly.

Truly hers was a wicked life. It meant nothing to her that God said, Thou shalt not commit adultery. Her great sin was to live with a man who was not her husband.

Jesus then went on to tell her about Himself as the promised Savior of mankind. Just as He said, *I that speak unto thee am He,* the disciples returned from the city with food, and asked Him to eat.

A great change seemed to come over the woman as she listened to Jesus. She felt the call to turn from her evil ways and begin a new life. A man who knew her sins as Jesus did and still promised salvation for her could be no other than the Messiah.

Then she left her water pot and hurried back to town. To all she met she said, *Come, see a man, who told me all things that ever I did: can this be the Christ?* They were surprised and hurried to Jacob's well.

Because of what the woman told, many believed He was the Christ and begged Him to stay with them. He stayed for two days teaching them God's Word. Many believed on Him and said to the woman, *Now we believe, not because of thy speaking: for we have heard for ourselves, and know that this is indeed the Savior of the world.* (This story is based on John 4:1-43.)

LESSON TEXT

Watch and pray, that ye enter not into temptation. Matthew 26:41.

HYMN (See page 141)

PRAYER

Purify me, O Lord, and I shall be clean;
Wash me, and I shall be whiter than snow. Amen.

BIBLE STUDY

1. Name the first five books of the Bible.
2. From which book is our story taken?
3. There are three small books called I John, II John, and III John. You will find them in the last part of the Bible. Look them up.
4. John also wrote the last book in the Bible. What is its name?
5. How many books of the Bible did John write? Name them.
6. Find John 4:25-26 and read it. What did the woman know of the promised Messiah?

QUESTIONS

1. What is the Sixth Commandment?
2. In the story, find the words of Jesus used when He told the woman of Samaria that she had broken this commandment. What is breaking the Sixth Commandment called?
3. Did she know better?
4. How did Jesus try to show her that He was the Messiah?
5. What proved to her that Jesus was the Christ? Find her words that tell us she believed Jesus was the Christ.
6. How long did Jesus stay in Sychar? Why did He stay?
7. How may we keep from breaking this and other commandments? (See the Lesson Text.)

The Samaritan Woman Tells About Jesus

Chapter 8

THE SEVENTH COMMANDMENT

Thou shalt not steal.

QUESTION: What does this mean?

ANSWER: We should fear and love God so that we do not rob our neighbor of his money or property, nor bring them into our possession by unfair dealing or fraud, but help him to improve and protect his property and living.

Samuel, the Honest Steward

SAMUEL, the prophet, had judged Israel for many years. Now he stood ready to give an account of his dealings with the people before he gave up his office to their first king, Saul. His conscience was clear but his heart was heavy with shame and sorrow. It was heavy with shame because his sons were not honest men who could take his place. It was heavy with sorrow because the people had used that as an excuse for asking for a king.

Let us try to picture the scene.

Samuel stood before his people, stately, grey-haired, kindly, and silent for a minute. He must have remembered all he had done for them. He had led them away from idol worship to the true God. He had led them against their enemies, the Philistines. He had been honest with them and had ruled them justly.

Perhaps he looked long at those who had offered him cattle and money if he would do as they wanted him to do. We may believe that those who had bribed his sons had tried to bribe him. But he had not taken bribes. It would have been easy to cheat them. But he did not stoop to that. Never had he tried to make himself rich nor tried to win the people's favor by dishonest deeds. His sons had been different. No one could say, however, that he had taught his sons to be dishonest.

His stern, quiet voice made everyone look at him as he spoke. He asked them whether they had anything against him. They all said before God and Saul that Samuel had never stolen from them, oppressed them, nor taken bribes.

This made the old leader happy and satisfied. He told them to obey God. As their leader he had led them in the ways of God

Samuel Crowns Saul King

and he could not bear to think that they might return to the evil ways of idol worship. Then he gave up his office with a clean record to the newly anointed king.

The people asked him to pray for them and he gladly did. (This story is based on I Samuel 12:1-5.)

LESSON TEXT

Nor thieves ... shall inherit the kingdom of God. I Corinthians 6:10.

HYMN (See page 141)

PRAYER

Dear Jesus, help me to be honest and true. Amen.

BIBLE STUDY

1. Name the books written by John.
2. How many New Testament books can you name in the order in which they come?
4. In the Old Testament are two books called I Samuel and II Samuel. Find them.
5. What book comes before I Samuel? And after II Samuel?
6. From what book is our story taken?

QUESTIONS

1. Who was Samuel? What was he trying to make the people see before he gave up his office?
2. Who had broken the Seventh Commandment? Why did it make Samuel unhappy?
3. What was the law about the Seventh Commandment at this time? (Exodus 22:1.)
4. What does God say to those who steal? (Lesson Text.)
5. Name the things that Samuel had done for the people.
6. Why did he want all to know that he left a clean record behind him as God's servant?
7. How did the people feel about him?
8. How did they show what they felt?
9. Why was Saul at this meeting?

Naboth and His Accusers

Chapter 9
THE EIGHTH COMMANDMENT

Thou shalt not bear false witness against thy neighbor.

QUESTION: What does this mean?

ANSWER: We should fear and love God so that we do not deceitfully belie, betray, backbite, nor slander our neighbor, but apologize for him, speak well of him, and put the most charitable construction on all that he does.

False Witness Against Naboth

NABOTH had a vineyard next to the palace of King Ahab who ruled in Samaria. Ahab was wicked in the sight of the Lord. Jezebel, his wife, often stirred him up to make trouble. Ahab worshipped idols and did all the things that Jezebel's people, the Phoenicians, did. Besides this he was very selfish.

Ahab wanted to make Naboth's vineyard into a vegetable garden for the palace. He offered Naboth another vineyard in place of his. *A better vineyard,* he said to tempt him. Naboth refused because the law of Moses said an Israelite must not part with his homestead. Ahab then wanted to give him money for it. Still Naboth refused, saying, *I will not give thee the inheritance of my fathers.* Naboth had the law of Moses on his side and he wanted to obey the law.

Can you imagine a king going to bed in a sullen fit of anger? That is what Ahab did. Very likely Jezebel comforted him, and said that Naboth was old-fashioned and unreasonable.

At last she demanded to know whether he was or was not the ruler of Israel. *Arise, and eat bread, and let thy heart be merry: I will give thee the vineyard!*

We can almost see her cruel face; how her eyes snapped and her lips curled in scorn at such a weakling. Her tight jaws plainly told that she was going to teach Naboth how dangerous it was to oppose the king's will.

If Naboth insisted on following the law, so would she. There was a law that she could use to get the vineyard. This law said that anyone who cursed God and the king must give up everything he had to the king. All she had to do was to prove that Naboth had cursed God and the king.

So Jezebel wrote letters to the officers and signed Ahab's name. In the letters she wrote, "Proclaim a fast and put Naboth before the people. Set two base men before him and let them say

Ahab and Jezebel

this against him: 'Thou didst curse God and the king!' Then carry him out and stone him to death."

When the cruel queen heard that the order had been carried out she hurried to Ahab. She told him that Naboth was dead and said: *Arise, take possession of the vineyard of Naboth.* And Ahab went to take possession.

But now God stepped in. He told Elijah to go and meet Ahab in the homestead that had been Naboth's. Elijah was one of the prophets that Jezebel had tried to kill. When Elijah met the king he brought him this message from God: *In the place where dogs licked the blood of Naboth shall dogs lick thy blood.... The dogs shall eat Jezebel.*

The cowardly Ahab tore his clothes, put sackcloth on his body, and ate no food. And everything happened as God had said. (This story is based on I Kings 21:1-16.)

LESSON TEXT

Wherefore, putting away falsehood, speak ye truth each one with his neighbor. Ephesians 4:25.

HYMN (See page 142)

PRAYER

Lord Jesus Christ, keep my heart and tongue free from lies, for Thy name's sake. Amen.

BIBLE STUDY

1. What four books come before I Kings?
2. What book comes after I Kings?
3. What book comes after Deuteronomy?
4. Name the five books before I Kings.
5. From which book is our story taken?
6. Find I Kings 21:5-19. Read it.

QUESTIONS

1. What is the Eighth Commandment?
2. What is another way of saying "false witness"? (See Catechism lesson.)
3. Who bore false witness against Naboth? How?
4. What other commandments did the king and queen break? When?
5. Why did Naboth refuse to sell the vineyard? (See Leviticus 25:23.)
6. Why did not Naboth disobey God's law and save his life?
7. Why was Ahab afraid?
8. How do we learn to keep the Commandments? (Hymn.)

Chapter 10

THE NINTH COMMANDMENT

Thou shalt not covet thy neighbor's house.

QUESTION: What does this mean?

ANSWER: We should fear and love God so that we do not seek by craftiness to gain possession of our neighbor's inheritance or home nor obtain them under pretense of a legal right, but assist and serve him in keeping the same.

THE TENTH COMMANDMENT

Thou shalt not covet thy neighbor's wife, nor his manservant, nor his maidservant, nor his cattle, nor anything that is thy neighbor's.

QUESTION: What does this mean?

ANSWER: We should fear and love God so that we do not estrange or entice away our neighbor's wife, servants, or cattle, but seek to have them remain and discharge their duty to him.

Gehazi, or the Sin of Covetousness

GEHAZI listened to what his master, Elisha, said to Naaman, captain of the Syrian army. He was surprised that Elisha refused ten talents of silver, six thousand pieces of gold, and ten changes of raiment. All this had been sent to pay Elisha for curing Naaman of leprosy.

God had given Elisha power to cure sick people. He loved to do God's work and would not take pay for it. When Elisha told Naaman to go in peace, Gehazi decided to get some of the money. His face could not have looked pleasant as he muttered these wicked words, *I will run after him, and take somewhat of him.*

When Naaman looked back, he saw Gehazi running after him. Naaman stepped from his chariot and greeted Gehazi with, *Is all well?* The greedy Gehazi answered, *All is well.* Then he told Naaman that two young men of the sons of the prophets had come to visit Elisha, and that Elisha wanted a talent of silver and two changes of clothing for them.

Elisha Refuses Naaman's Gift

Naaman was glad to give and urged him to accept two talents. He sent two servants to help Gehazi carry the money and clothes. When they came to the hill Gehazi let the servants go back to Naaman. He carried the gifts into the house and hid them. Then he went to Elisha as if nothing had happened.

But Elisha knew. He said, *Whence comest thou, Gehazi?* Now was Gehazi's time to confess but he did not. Surely his conscience must have hurt him when he answered, *Thy servant went no whither.*

Then Elisha again spoke, *Went not my heart with thee, when the man turned from his chariot to meet thee? Is it a time to receive money, and to receive garments, and oliveyards and vineyards, and sheep and oxen, and men-servants and maid-servants? The leprosy therefore of Naaman shall cleave unto thee, and unto thy seed for ever.*

And Gehazi went out from the presence of Elisha a leper as white as snow. (This story is based on II Kings 5:20-27.)

LESSON TEXT

Take heed, and keep yourselves from all covetousness. Luke 12:15.

HYMN (See page 142)

PRAYER

God, teach me to be a good steward. Help me to use according to Thy will what I have now or ever will have. Amen.

BIBLE STUDY

1. What are the names of the two books that come after II Kings?
2. Name the books from Joshua to II Chronicles.
3. I Kings and II Kings tell the story of Israel's kings from the death of David to the last king who was brought to Babylon as a captive.
4. I Chronicles and II Chronicles tell the religious history of Israel to the return from the captivity in Babylon.
5. Find II Kings 5:20-27. Read it.
6. Read II Kings 5:14-17. What do these verses tell?

QUESTIONS

1. Why did Elisha refuse the money?
2. What chance did Gehazi have to be a God-fearing man?
3. Into what other sins did covetousness lead Gehazi?
4. Did Gehazi suffer alone for his sins?
5. Whom do you harm beside yourself when you sin?
6. How can we be saved from the leprosy of sin?
7. What does Numbers 32:23 say about sin?

Chapter 11

GOD'S DECLARATION CONCERNING HIS COMMANDMENTS

QUESTION: What does God declare concerning all these Commandments?

ANSWER: He says: I the Lord thy God am a jealous God, visiting the iniquity of the fathers upon the children unto the third and fourth generation of them that hate Me; and showing mercy unto thousands of them that love Me and keep My commandments.

QUESTION: What does this mean?

ANSWER: God threatens to punish all who transgress these commandments. We should, therefore, fear His wrath, and in no wise disobey them. But He promises grace and every blessing to all who keep them. We should, therefore, love Him, trust in Him, and gladly keep His commandments.

Punishments and Blessings

THE commandments we have studied are God's laws, and God's laws are always working. If we obey God we will in some way reap blessing. If we disobey, punishment in some form will overtake us. An honest man will have the blessing of an upright character. A thief is cursed with a dishonest character. Obedience to God gives a good conscience and a good conscience is one of the greatest blessings in life. Disobedience to God brings a bad conscience and a bad conscience is a burden and a curse to any person.

Obedience to God also brings blessing to children and children's children, while disobedience brings punishment. Abraham trusted and obeyed God, and God blessed not only him but also his descendants. Through Abraham's people God sent Christ. Cain and his descendants persisted in disobeying God and the Flood came.

There was a heathen woman who became an obedient believer in God and God blessed both her and her descendants. Her name was Ruth.

It was in the days of the Judges in Israel. There was a great famine in the land and a man and his wife, Naomi, and their two

Ruth Refuses to Leave Naomi

sons went to the land of Moab, east of the Dead Sea. Not long afterward the man died, but the family did not go back to their own country. The sons married and settled down in Moab. The name of the girls they married were Orpah and Ruth.

After some years the sons, too, died and Naomi decided to go back to her own people. Orpah and Ruth said they would go with her. They had learned to respect her so highly and love her so dearly that they would not part from her. Naomi must have been a very fine and sensible woman to win so fully the love of her daughters-in-law.

The three women started on the journey, but Naomi was troubled in her mind. She did not think it was right that Orpah and Ruth should leave their own people. She urged them to go back and said to them, *Go, return each of you to her mother's house: the Lord deal kindly with you, as ye have dealt with the dead and with me.*

Orpah was finally persuaded to return, but Ruth refused. Her love for her mother-in-law was stronger than even her love for her nearest relatives. Besides, she had come to believe in her mother-in-law's God and wanted to serve Him and belong to His people. She clung to Naomi and said, *Whither thou goest, I will go; and where thou lodgest, I will lodge; thy people shall be my people, and thy God my God; where thou diest, will I die; and there will I be buried.*

The two women continued their journey and finally came to Bethlehem, the home town of Naomi. There Ruth later married Boaz and became the great-grandmother of David. Mary, the mother of Jesus, was of the family of David and so Ruth became one of the ancestors of Jesus Christ.

I the Lord thy God am a jealous God ... showing mercy unto thousands of them that love me and keep my commandments. (This story is based on Ruth 1; 2; 4:13-17.)

LESSON TEXT

I the Lord thy God am a jealous God, visiting the iniquity of the fathers upon the children, upon the third and upon the fourth generation of them that hate Me, and showing lovingkindness unto thousands of them that love Me and keep My commandments. Exodus 20:5-6.

HYMN (See page 142)

PRAYER

Dear God and Father, help me to love Thee and to keep Thy commandments. Let Thy goodness go with me and with all Thy people. Amen.

BIBLE STUDY

1. Where in the Bible is the Book of Ruth?
2. Name the first fourteen books of the Bible.
3. Find Exodus 20:5-6. Read it.
4. Look up Ruth 1:15-18. Read it.

QUESTIONS

1. How did God bless Abraham and his descendants?
2. What is it that brings a bad conscience?
3. Who was Ruth?
4. What kind of woman was Naomi?
5. Why did not Naomi become like the heathen Moabites the many years she lived among them?
6. Why did Ruth refuse to leave her mother-in-law?
7. Repeat what Ruth answered Naomi.
8. What part of the Lesson Text was fulfilled upon Ruth?
9. How was it fulfilled?

The Creed

THE FIRST ARTICLE—OF CREATION

I believe in God the Father almighty, Maker of heaven and earth.

THE SECOND ARTICLE—OF REDEMPTION

And in Jesus Christ His only Son, our Lord; who was conceived by the Holy Spirit, born of the Virgin Mary; suffered under Pontius Pilate, was crucified, dead, and buried; He descended into hell; the third day He rose again from the dead; He ascended into heaven, and sitteth on the right hand of God the Father almighty; from thence He shall come to judge the quick and the dead.

THE THIRD ARTICLE—OF SANCTIFICATION

I believe in the Holy Spirit; the holy Christian Church, the Communion of Saints; the forgiveness of sins; the resurrection of the body; and the life everlasting. Amen.

THE FIRST ARTICLE — OF CREATION

I believe in God the Father almighty, Maker of heaven and earth.

QUESTION: What does this mean?

ANSWER: I believe that God has created me and all that exists; that He has given and still preserves to me my body and soul, my eyes and ears, and all my members, my reason and all the powers of my soul, together with food and raiment, home and family, and all my property; that He daily provides abundantly for all the needs of my life, protects me from all danger, and guards and keeps me from all evil; and that He does this purely out of fatherly and divine goodness and mercy, without any merit or worthiness in me; for all of which I am in duty bound to thank, praise, serve, and obey Him. This is most certainly true.

THE SECOND ARTICLE — OF REDEMPTION

And in Jesus Christ His only Son, our Lord; who was conceived by the Holy Spirit, born of the Virgin Mary; suffered under Pontius Pilate, was crucified, dead, and buried; He descended into hell; the third day He rose again from the dead; He ascended into heaven, and sitteth on the right hand of God the Father almighty; from thence He shall come to judge the quick and the dead.

QUESTION: What does this mean?

ANSWER: I believe that Jesus Christ, true God, begotten of the Father from eternity, and also true Man, born of the Virgin Mary, is my Lord; Who has redeemed me, a lost and condemned creature, bought me and freed me from all sins, from death, and from the power of the devil; not with silver and gold, but with His holy and precious blood, and with His innocent sufferings and death; in order that I might be His own, live under Him in His kingdom, and serve Him in everlasting righteousness, innocence, and blessedness; even as He is risen from the dead, and lives and reigns to all eternity. This is most certainly true.

THE THIRD ARTICLE — OF SANCTIFICATION

I believe in the Holy Spirit; the holy Christian Church, the Communion of Saints; the forgiveness of sins; the resurrection of the body; and the life everlasting. Amen.

QUESTION: What does this mean?

ANSWER: I believe that I cannot by my own reason or strength believe in Jesus Christ my Lord, or come to Him; but the Holy Spirit has called me through the Gospel, enlightened me with His gifts, and sanctified and preserved me in the true faith; in like manner as He calls, gathers, enlightens, and sanctifies the whole Christian Church on earth, and preserves it in union with Jesus Christ in the one true faith; in which Christian Church He daily forgives abundantly all my sins, and the sins of all believers, and at the last day will raise up me and all the dead, and will grant everlasting life to me and to all who believe in Christ. This is most certainly true.

Zacharias Sprinkles Incense

Chapter 12

THE FIRST ARTICLE — OF CREATION

I believe that God has created me and all that exists; that He has given and still preserves to me my body and soul, my eyes and ears, and all my members, my reason and all the powers of my soul. . . .

Zacharias

ZACHARIAS was a priest. His wife's name was Elisabeth. They were an old couple, righteous before God, but often sad because they had no children.

Zacharias was now in the temple at Jerusalem doing the duties of the priest. When the bell tinkled the priests took their places throughout the temple courts. Zacharias and his assistant began their duties too. The helper took the coals from the golden firepan that he carried, laid them on the altar, and went out. Zacharias sprinkled the incense on the glowing coals. As the perfumed clouds rose upward, he joined his prayers with those of the people. There were many things to pray for besides his daily prayer for a child.

As he prayed he saw an angel before him on the right side of the altar. *And Zacharias was troubled when he saw him, and fear fell upon him.* But the archangel, Gabriel—for it was he—told him not to fear. He promised Zacharias a son, a wonderful son. He was to be the forerunner of Christ and Zacharias must name him John.

That Christ was coming, Zacharias could believe, but that he and Elisabeth would have a son he could not believe. When he asked for a sign whereby he might know that this was true, a sudden dumbness struck him. When he tried to speak he could not.

Meanwhile the people waited for him to come out to bless them in the name of the Lord and dismiss them. But Zacharias could not finish his services. He came out at last as if in a daze. He made signs to let the people know that God had spoken to him.

In due season the child was born. As was the custom of the Jews, he was circumcised on the eighth day and given a name. A dispute arose over his name, for the relatives wanted to call him Zacharias after his father. Elisabeth said he should be named John. Zacharias agreed with her by writing on a tablet: *His name is John.* At once his tongue was loosed, and his voice came back to him. He spoke and praised God. He had learned to trust in the almighty God.

Because John was born of a priestly line he should have gone into training for the priesthood. But Zacharias remembered what the angel Gabriel had said. John was to be a prophet like Elijah. So the father let him go into the desert. Here he lived while God trained him for the work he should do. (This story is based on Luke 1:5-24 and 57-80.)

LESSON TEXT

In Him we live, and move, and have our being. Acts 17:28.

HYMN (See page 142)

PRAYER

Dear Lord, help me to take Thee at Thy word, for Thou art almighty and faithful. Amen.

BIBLE STUDY

1. Name the first four books of the New Testament.
2. What book comes after these four?
3. Who was Luke? (See Bible Study in Chapter 5.)
4. Read Luke 1:17. What should be John's work?
5. Read Matthew 3:1-3 and John 1:23. How did John begin his work?
6. Find Isaiah 12:2 and read it.

QUESTIONS

1. Who were Zacharias and Elisabeth?
2. What were Zacharias' temple duties?
3. These are some of the things for which Zacharias prayed:
   a. that God would forgive his and the nation's sins
   b. that God would accept the atonement of the lamb that was to be burned on the altar
   c. that God would soon send the Messiah or the promised Savior
   d. that God would give him a son (see Luke 1:13)
4. What part of Gabriel's message did Zacharias believe?
5. What happened because he did not trust in God's promise?
6. Why did a dispute arise about the baby's name?
7. Where did John get his training? (The desert of Judea, between Kedron and the Dead Sea. Locate it.)

Zacharias Writes His Son's Name

Chapter 13

THE FIRST ARTICLE — OF CREATION

I believe that God ... has given and still preserves to me ... food and raiment, home and family, and all my property. ...

God Blesses Abraham

ONE day a man came running to Abraham, who at that time lived in the southern part of Canaan. The man had traveled far and was greatly excited. He told that four enemy kings had captured the people in Sodom and Gomorrah, and that Lot and his family were also among the prisoners.

The news stirred Abraham to go at once to the rescue because Lot was his brother's son. Though old, Abraham was still strong and would himself lead his men in the pursuit. He asked his three Amorite friends to join him.

They started early in the morning and marched rapidly all day. Towards evening they came near the enemy's camp. Abraham divided his men. At the given hour that night they attacked the camp from different sides.

It was too dark for the trapped kings and their men to see how many were upon them, neither could they tell friend from foe. They fled in such haste and terror that they left all their goods, captive women, and children behind them. Abraham's men pursued them a long way to make sure they would not return.

On the way home Abraham passed through Shaveh. Here Melchizedek, king of Salem (Jerusalem), who was a priest of God, met him. He brought Abraham bread and wine and blessed him. In return Abraham gave him a tenth of all.

The king of Sodom also met him at Shaveh. He too was grateful and wanted to pay the great leader who had saved his people. He wanted to give Abraham all the goods and asked to keep only the people. By the law of the land the goods belonged to the rescuer; but Abraham would not take anything. He said: *I will not take a thread nor a shoe-latchet, nor aught that is thine, lest thou shouldest say, "I have made Abram rich."*

All Abraham asked for was the share of the goods that belonged to his Amorite friends. He was rich already, but it was God who had given him his riches. He would not take anything

Abraham Praises God

that would tie him to the people of the country. He was to live his life apart from them and to trust in God alone.

After Abraham had returned to his home God spoke to him again. It was night and pointing to the stars God said: *Look now toward heaven, and number the stars, if thou be able to number them: and He said unto him, So shall thy seed be.*

And Abraham believed the Lord. (This story is based on Genesis 14.)

LESSON TEXT

Fear not, Abram: I am thy shield, and thy exceeding great reward. Genesis 15:1.

HYMN (See page 142)

PRAYER

Dear God, daily give us what we need for this body and life. Help us to believe that Thou wilt take care of us. Help us to be thankful. Amen.

BIBLE STUDY

1. Genesis means origin, creation. The Book of Genesis tells of the beginning of the world and of the people of Israel.
2. Exodus means a going out. The Book of Exodus tells of the people of Israel going out of Egypt.
3. Leviticus is from the word Levite. The Levites were the priests and their helpers. The Book of Leviticus gives the laws for the priests.
4. Numbers tells of the numbering of Israel. Therefore the name.
5. Deuteronomy means the second law. In this book Moses repeats the law to the people of Israel.
6. Find Genesis 14:21-24. Read it.

QUESTIONS

1. Who spoke the words of our Lesson Text? To whom? Why?
2. Who was Lot? What had happened to him?
3. Can you describe the attack on the camp?
4. How many were glad that Abraham had defeated the four kings?
5. How did the king of Sodom show his gratefulness to Abraham?
6. What did Abraham say to the king?
7. Why did Abraham refuse the king's gifts?
8. What was God's message to Abraham?
9. What words in the First Article mean the same?
10. What reward could Abraham have had right away?
11. Why was he wise in refusing it?

Chapter 14

THE FIRST ARTICLE — OF CREATION

I believe that God . . . daily provides abundantly for all the needs of my life, protects me from all danger, and guards and keeps me from all evil; and that He does this purely out of fatherly and divine goodness and mercy, without any merit or worthiness in me; for all of which I am in duty bound to thank, praise, serve, and obey Him. This is most certainly true.

Peter's Escape from Prison

PETER, bound with two chains, lay asleep between two soldiers behind a prison door guarded by keepers. Herod had jailed him because he preached about Jesus Christ. Herod knew that the Jews liked to have him persecute the Christians, so he put the disciples into prison. Many of the things Peter said must have made Herod feel guilty.

These things did not worry Peter. He slept even though he was in prison. He trusted in God to keep him. He had gone to sleep with a prayer on his lips and he knew that the members of the new church were praying for him too. He believed that as long as God had work for him to do here on earth, He would protect him. When that work was over, he would gladly die and go to be with Christ. And so he slept peacefully.

Suddenly he sat up bewildered. What had struck his side? What made the prison light? Who was it that told him to rise and make ready to leave the prison? It was an angel who had awakened him.

In obedient wonder Peter followed the angel past the first and second guards to the iron gate that led into the city. Peter was astonished when the gate opened by itself. He followed on into the street. There

Peter in Prison

The Angel Leads Peter Out of Prison

he found himself alone. Very likely he stood for a moment not knowing just what to do. Soon he understood that God wanted him to move on to freedom. He became sure of himself.

He sped away into the darkness—not afraid, but in a great hurry. He came to a stop at the door of the house where the Christians were praying for him. This house was the home of the mother of John Mark and had long been the Christian meeting house. Peter had often been here.

The maid who answered his knock was so surprised that she forgot to open the door. When she brought the news inside to the others they said that she was out of her mind. Peter kept on knocking until they opened the door. He motioned them to keep quiet.

Hurriedly he told them how he had escaped. No need for them to question his safety or doubt God's protection of His children. Here stood the living Peter as proof, if they needed proof.

Peter was free, but he could not stay here long. He said goodbye to his friends and in God's name went out into the night again to a place where Herod could not reach him. We may be sure that wherever he went he praised God and told how mighty He is to protect His children in all sorts of danger. (This story is based on Acts 12:1-19.)

LESSON TEXT

The Lord is my helper; I will not fear. Hebrews 13:6.

HYMN (See page 142)

PRAYER

Heavenly Father, I thank Thee that Thou art watching over Thy children and taking care of them. Teach me to trust Thee and to love and obey Thee. Amen.

BIBLE STUDY

1. Where in the Bible is the Book of Acts?
2. Name the book that goes before it and the one that comes after it.
3. Acts tells of the acts or work of the apostles and their helpers in spreading the Gospel.
4. Find the Epistle to the Hebrews.
5. This epistle (letter) was written to Christian Hebrews, that is to Christian Jews.
6. The story today is based on Acts 12:1-19. Find it.

QUESTIONS

1. Where is Peter in this lesson? Why?
2. Why could he sleep though he was in prison and his life was in danger? (Lesson Text.)
3. Who awakened him? How?
4. What did the angel do when they were out of the prison?
5. Why did Peter go to the house of Mark's mother after the angel left him?
6. Why did not his friends believe he was at the door?
7. Are we ever called upon to suffer for Christ even though we do not go to prison? (Yes, in taking a stand for Christ.) How can we meet such suffering and be happy in it? (Loving Christ, prayer, and trust in our heavenly Father.)

The Maid Answers Peter's Knock

Chapter 15
THE SECOND ARTICLE — OF REDEMPTION

I believe that Jesus Christ, true God, begotten of the Father from eternity, and also true Man, born of the Virgin Mary, is my Lord. . . .

The First Christmas

THE first Christmas came with the birth of Jesus. On His birthday we rejoice by singing praises to God, holding special services, and giving gifts—much as the shepherds did when the angels told them Jesus was born.

Jesus was born in Bethlehem, eighty miles south from Nazareth, which was the home of His parents, Mary and Joseph. They had come to Bethlehem to register because the ruler, Caesar Augustus, wanted all the people to enroll for the census he was taking in order to tax them. Each one registered where the home of his ancestors had been. Because both Joseph and Mary were related to David, they came to Bethlehem of Judea where David had lived.

When they came to the city they found no place to stay. Many strangers had come in before them. At last Joseph found a place and led tired Mary into it. It was not much of a place—a stable cut into the limestone hillside. Here the Christ Child was born and laid in a manger filled with hay and straw for the cattle.

That night there were shepherds keeping watch over their sheep on the same hillsides where David had tended his flocks. An angel came to them, and the glory of the heavens lighted up the place about them. The angel said, *Be not afraid; . . . for there is born to you this day in the city of David a Savior, who is Christ the Lord.* Then a host of angels joined the one and they all praised God saying, *Glory to God in the highest, and on earth peace among men in whom He is well pleased.*

When the heavenly choir faded away into the night the shepherds decided to go to find the holy Child that it had pleased God to tell them about. In a manger in Bethlehem they found Him, wrapped in swaddling clothes, the sign whereby the angels said they would know Him. They worshipped Him and very likely offered Him gifts of what little they had,—milk, cheese, wool,

The Shepherds at the Manger

and perhaps even a little lamb. But the gifts were great because their love was great.

They knew this Baby was no ordinary baby. The angels had told them He was the Messiah their nation had been waiting for. They did not look down on Him because of His lowly birthplace. They were lowly themselves. Their great king, David, had also been a lowly shepherd.

The shepherds praised God that the Lord Himself had come to save His people, and the rest of the world. They told Mary, Joseph, and everyone they met what the angel had told them about Jesus. We can almost see them go out of their way to find people to whom to tell the Christmas story. On their way back to their sheep they rejoiced and praised God for all they had heard and seen, perhaps singing their praises in the words of the angels' song, *Glory to God in the highest!* (This story is based on Luke 2:2-21.)

LESSON TEXT

There is born to you this day in the city of David a Savior, who is Christ, the Lord. Luke 2:11.

HYMN (See page 142)

PRAYER

Glory and praise to Thee, Lord Jesus Christ, that Thou art our Lord and our Savior. Help us always to love and serve Thee. Amen.

BIBLE STUDY

1. Name the first five books in the New Testament.
2. Name the books written by John.
3. Read Matthew 1:21-22. What do these verses tell?
4. Find Luke 2:2-21 and read it.

QUESTIONS

1. When was the first Christmas?
2. In what way was the first Christmas like our Christmas?
3. Why was Jesus born in Bethlehem and not in Nazareth?
4. How did the shepherds know Jesus was born?
5. By what sign did they find him? (Luke 2:7.)
6. Where did they find the holy Child?
7. How did they worship Him? (Two ways.)
8. When you read the words, "First Christmas," what picture do you see? If you see more than one picture, describe them all.

Jesus and the Blind Man

Chapter 16

THE SECOND ARTICLE — OF REDEMPTION

I believe that Jesus Christ, true God, begotten of the Father from eternity, and also true Man, born of the Virgin Mary, is my Lord. . . .

The Man Born Blind

ONE day a beggar, blind from birth, sat near the gate of the temple. Truly he was a pitiful sight—shut up in the dark by himself, never knowing the light of the sun except to feel it warm his rag-clad body. As he walked he often stumbled. He felt his way over the ground where other men walked, always hoping that some kind person would give him just a little help.

Now Jesus, who had been teaching within the temple, came

The Blind Man Sees

out and saw him. The disciples, too, saw him and asked, *Rabbi, who sinned, this man, or his parents, that he should be born blind? Jesus answered, Neither did this man sin, nor his parents: but that the works of God should be made manifest in him. We must work the works of Him that sent me... When I am in the world, I am the light of the world.*

The beggar listened intently as he heard footsteps near him. Maybe he wondered what was happening when Jesus spat on the clay and softened it. He must have been startled when the clay was laid on his eyes and a kind voice told him to go and wash in the pool of Siloam. He went and came back seeing.

Here was help such as he had never dreamed of. The neighbors crowded around him. What had happened? How? Who was the healer? The beggar told them what had happened to him. They hustled him to the Pharisees to find out what they thought about it. He listened to them argue about Jesus. They asked the beggar what he thought about Jesus and he answered, *He is a prophet.*

But the Pharisees were not satisfied. They called the beggar's parents and asked if this was their son, who had been born blind. Yes, he was their son, but more they dared not say for fear that they might be forbidden to come into the synagogue to worship.

Again the Pharisees turned to the man and asked for his story. He answered without fear, *I told you even now, and ye did not hear; wherefore would ye hear it again? Would ye also become His disciples?* That made them angry and they cursed him and threw him out.

When Jesus heard how the beggar had been treated He came to him. Many words may have passed between them, but the Bible records only Jesus' question, *Dost thou believe on the Son of God?* The beggar asked, *And who is He, Lord, that I may believe on Him?* Then Jesus said, *Thou hast both seen Him, and He it is that speaketh with thee.*

A new and happy light leaped into the once blind eyes. Deeply moved he answered, *Lord, I believe.* And he fell down and worshipped Jesus, the Son of God, the Light of the World. (This story is based on John 9.)

LESSON TEXT

Lord, I believe. John 9:38.

HYMN (See page 142)

PRAYER

Abide, our pathway brighten
With Thy celestial ray,
Blest light our souls enlighten
Show us the truth, the way. Amen.

BIBLE STUDY

1. Repeat the names of the books written by John.
2. Look up the four books that follow after the Gospel according to John and name them.
3. Name the four Gospels.
4. Each Gospel tells the story of Jesus Christ.
5. Turn to John 9:35-38 and read it to find out how the blind man learned to believe in Jesus as the Son of God.

QUESTIONS

1. How did the beggar meet Jesus?
2. What did Jesus do for him? How?
3. Why did the neighbors rush him to the Pharisees?
4. What did the Pharisees think of the cure?
5. How did the beggar stand by Christ? How did Christ claim him?
6. Why did the parents refuse to speak up for Christ?
7. Why did the Pharisees become angry with the beggar?
8. When did the beggar find out who Jesus was?
9. How does the Lesson Text fit the Second Article?
10. Learn the hymn.

Chapter 17

THE SECOND ARTICLE — OF REDEMPTION

I believe that Jesus Christ . . . has redeemed me, a lost and condemned creature, bought me and freed me from all sins, from death, and from the power of the devil; not with silver and gold, but with His holy and precious blood, and with His innocent sufferings and death. . . .

The Suffering and Death of Jesus

THE three cross-bearers were on their way to Golgotha. Each was guarded by soldiers. A hissing crowd followed them. The cruel jeers fell mostly on the central figure, Jesus. He staggered and fell. He had lived His whole life in the shadow of this Cross. Why should He fall under it now?

He had been stripped of His clothes, His hands had been tied and He had been so bound to the stake that His back had missed not one of the thirty-nine strokes from the lead-laden whips. After that it had been hard to stand up like a king, for as such they hailed Him, "The King of the Jews!" We can almost see how His bleeding, welted body had tried to withdraw from the coarse, purple robe. His trembling hand had grasped the mock sceptre, a common reed.

Without a word He had endured the soldiers' spitting, kicking, and rough jokes while they rigged Him up as a king. Then they had led Him to Pilate who had turned Him over to the yelling, blood-thirsty mob, screaming like madmen for His crucifixion. Since His arrest in Gethsemane He had stood trial for blasphemy or for claiming to be a king, before Caiaphas, Pilate, Herod, and again before Pilate. And Pilate had turned Him over to the crowd in place of the robber, Barabbas.

Is it any wonder Jesus fell beneath the burden of the Cross? "Crucify Him!" still rang in His ears as Simon unwillingly took the cross from Him. Jesus struggled to His feet. He stumbled forward, going the way of the cross for you and for me. Let us not forget that besides the bodily sufferings He carried the burden of our sins. That was the heaviest part of the load.

On the cross He cried, *My God, My God, why hast Thou forsaken me?* People had already left Him, but now even God left Him. Alone, He had to suffer for the sins of men.

Jesus Finds the Disciples Asleep

The moment death came He cried, *It is finished!* Then, in a triumphant voice, *Father, into thy hands I commend my spirit.* Thus He died. (This story is based on Luke 23:33-46.)

LESSON TEXT

It is finished. John 19:30.

HYMN (See page 142)

PRAYER

Jesus Christ, I thank Thee that Thou didst suffer and die for my sins. Amen.

BIBLE STUDY

1. Name the first eight books of the New Testament.
2. What is the name of the little book between III John and Revelation?
3. Name the last five books in the New Testament.
4. What does the Book of Acts tell?
5. Find John 19:30 and explain what Jesus meant.
6. The story today is based on Luke 23:33-46. Find it and read it.

QUESTIONS

1. Who said the words of our Lesson Text?
2. What was finished?
3. How did Jesus die? Only the Romans crucified people alive.
4. Can you tell what blasphemy means? Why did they charge Jesus with blasphemy? Luke 22:67-71 for help.
5. Why did Jesus fall under His cross?
6. How did the soldiers mock Him?
7. How did Jesus bear this cruel treatment? Why?
8. Find the places that show that Jesus did not think about Himself.
9. When did Jesus suffer most? Why?
10. Why did God forsake Him?
11. What do you think this means: A bleeding Christ; a pleading Christ; a leading Christ?

Chapter 18

THE SECOND ARTICLE — OF REDEMPTION

I believe that Jesus Christ . . . has redeemed me . . . bought me and freed me . . . in order that I might be His own, live under Him in His kingdom, and serve Him in everlasting righteousness, innocence, and blessedness; even as He is risen from the dead, and lives and reigns to all eternity. This is most certainly true.

The Risen Christ

THE body of Jesus lay in the rock-hewn tomb while His soul went to His Father in heaven. He also appeared in hell showing His victory over death and the devil.

Early Sunday morning the ground suddenly quaked. An angel from God descended from heaven and rolled away the stone from the door of the grave. His appearance was as lightning and his dress as white as snow. The guards were so frightened that they fell to the ground as dead men. The Lord burst the gates of death and rose on the third day as He had said that He would.

Jesus at once began to comfort and help His disciples and friends. Their hearts were filled with sorrow and they were greatly confused. Was not Jesus the promised Messiah? Had He deceived them? It seemed impossible. Still, He had been put to death and buried. How could the enemies have crucified Him if He were Messiah, God's almighty Son? Their faith in Him had been destroyed, their hope crushed.

The women came to the grave early Easter morning to anoint His body. They were looking for a corpse. They found the living Lord.

Angels were the first to bring the surprising news that Jesus was risen. But the disciples would not believe it. Then Jesus Himself came to them.

He appeared first to Mary Magdalene, from whom He had cast out seven demons. Then He showed Himself to some of the other women who had been following Him. He also appeared to Peter on that first Easter Sunday.

That same day Jesus came and walked with two of His friends on their way to Emmaus. He listened to the sad story they told

Mary at the Tomb

of the death of their leader. Then He explained to them what the Old Testament Scriptures said. Christ should suffer, die, and rise again. Though they felt as they used to when Jesus talked to them, they did not know Him. They asked Him to stay with them and He did. When they sat down to eat, He took the bread, blessed it, brake it, and gave it to them as He had done so often. In a flash they knew Him and just as quickly He vanished. But they had seen Him alive and their faith in Him had been restored.

Still the day's work was not over. In the evening ten of the disciples and others were together at a house in Jerusalem. Peter was telling how the Lord had appeared to him. The two on the Emmaus road had returned and reported how He had walked with them and how they knew Him.

Then suddenly Jesus Himself stood in the midst of them. His first words were, *Peace be unto you.* They were afraid and thought they saw a ghost. Then He showed them the marks in His hands and feet. Even so they did not believe that He was the risen Lord. They still thought it was a ghost. So He took a piece of a broiled fish and ate in order to prove that He was a living person.

During the following forty days Jesus showed Himself again and again to His disciples and friends. He taught them, comforted them, and convinced them that He was truly risen from the dead. Thus He restored their faith in Him.

When the time came that He should ascend to His Father, He called them together on the slopes of the Mount of Olives. He spoke to them as a father speaks to his children when leaving them for a little while. Raising His nail-pierced hands He blessed them and rose into heaven. Now all doubts had disappeared. They fell down and worshipped Him.

While yet they looked into the sky where He had disappeared, two men in white stood beside them saying, *This Jesus, who was received up from you into heaven, shall so come in like manner as ye beheld Him going into heaven.* (This story is based on Mark 16:9-14.)

LESSON TEXT

He is not here, but is risen. Luke 24:6.

HYMN (See page 142)

PRAYER

Based on the Bible Study.

BIBLE STUDY

1. How did the risen Lord prove that He was the same? Read Luke 24:39-40 and John 20:27.
2. Did He know His friends? Read John 20:16 and 21:15-17.
3. Read Luke 24:15, 16, 30, 31, 36; John 20:14-16 and 19; John 21:4-7; I Corinthians 15:40. Explain what kind of body the risen Lord had.
4. Did the Lord appear only to His disciples and friends or did He also appear to others? (Read I Corinthians 15:5-8.)
5. What did Jesus prove by His resurrection? (See Romans 1:4.)
6. What good would our faith in Christ do us if He were not risen? (Read I Corinthians 15:14 and 17-19.)
7. How does the Bible assure us that we also shall rise from the dead? (Read Acts 26:23 and I Corinthians 15:12, 20, 21, 22, 23.)

QUESTIONS

1. What is the Lesson Text? Who said it? To whom was it spoken?
2. How long was Jesus in the grave?
3. Why was the grave sealed and guarded?
4. Why could Jesus rise from the dead?
5. How long was Jesus on earth after He arose? (Forty days.)
6. What was His work during that time? How did He do that work? Why was it necessary that He do it? (Bible reference John 20:21.)
7. When did the disciples fully believe He was risen?
8. Find the sentence in the story that tells when they fully believed.
9. Find the part that tells He is coming in person to earth again.
10. How is He coming when He comes again? What is He coming for? (Second Article.)
11. Why did He want the disciples to see Him ascend?
12. What effect did the ascension have on them?

Chapter 19

THE THIRD ARTICLE — OF SANCTIFICATION

I believe that I cannot by my own reason or strength believe in Jesus Christ my Lord, or come to Him; but the Holy Spirit has called me through the Gospel, enlightened me with His gifts, and sanctified and preserved me in the true faith; in like manner as He calls, gathers, enlightens, and sanctifies the whole Christian Church on earth, and preserves it in union with Jesus Christ in the one true faith. . . .

Pentecost

FIFTY days had passed since the resurrection and it was Pentecost again. People from every land were in Jerusalem to celebrate the great Jewish holiday. Pentecost was their feast of the harvest. Sometimes it was called the Feast of First Fruits. Early harvest was over by that time, and many were free to come to the celebration.

As bands of men, women, and children neared the city, many fell to their knees, lifted their hands to heaven, and burst into songs of praise to God. Priests in white robes came to meet them, joined the pilgrims in their song, and escorted them through the gates into the city, through the streets, and to the temple.

At the temple hill each one put his basket on his shoulder and marched in line into the Court of Men. Here the Levites, playing and singing, joined the procession. The doves were handed to the priests as burnt-offerings and the first-fruits of the harvest were given over at the altar as ordered by the Mosaic law. Then the pilgrims went to stay with relatives or friends.

The disciples, too, were in Jerusalem staying with friends. They had been here since the ascension, ten days ago. They did not think about the temple services as much as they did about Christ and His promise to send them the Holy Spirit.

This day they were together praying and talking as usual. *Suddenly there came from heaven a sound as of the rushing of a mighty wind, . . . And there appeared unto them tongues parting asunder, like as of fire; and it sat upon each one of them.*

Others in the city heard the rushing sound. They hurried to the house where the disciples were. They wondered among themselves at what they saw and heard. The disciples were praising

The Disciples Praising God

God in different languages so that each one who listened heard the language of his home country. Some mocked them and said they were drunk on new wine.

Then Peter stood up and spoke to the people. They listened to him for they were anxious to find out what all this meant. He told them that what they saw had been foretold by the prophet Joel, who said, *I will pour forth of my spirit upon all flesh.*

He did not need to teach them the Old Testament for they were devout men; but he had to teach them that Jesus Christ was the Savior promised in the Old Testament. Peter proved to them that Jesus was the Messiah they had prayed and waited for—and then crucified! It frightened them. They cried in their distress, *Brethren, what shall we do?* Peter told them to repent of their sins and be baptized.

About three thousand were baptized. This was the beginning of the Christian church. (This story is based on Acts 2:1-8.)

LESSON TEXT

I will pour out my Spirit upon all flesh; and your sons and your daughters shall prophesy. Joel 2:28.

HYMN (See page 142)

PRAYER

O Holy Spirit, fill us with Thy power. Cleanse us and make us Christ-like. Amen.

BIBLE STUDY

1. Where in the Old Testament do we have the Minor Prophets?
2. How many were they? (See Bible Study in Chapter 6.)
3. Find the Book of Joel.
4. What book goes before it and what comes after it?
5. Read Joel 2:28-29.
6. Your story is based on Acts 2:1-8. Find it and read it.

QUESTIONS

1. Why did the Jews keep Pentecost? How? Where? When?
2. Why were the disciples in Jerusalem? (Acts 1:4-6.)
3. What promise had Christ made them? (See references for question 2.)
4. How was the promise fulfilled? When?
5. What did Peter have to teach them?
6. Why is Pentecost called the birthday of the church?
7. Why may we call them the first-fruits of the seed sown by Jesus?

Mary Anoints Jesus' Feet

Chapter 20

THE THIRD ARTICLE — OF SANCTIFICATION

I believe that . . . the Holy Spirit . . . in the Christian Church . . . daily forgives abundantly all my sins. . . .

A Sinner Saved

SIMON, a Pharisee, had invited Jesus to dine with him. While they were eating a sinful woman of the street came in. She was looking for Jesus. When she saw Him she walked noiselessly across the room until she stood behind His feet. Then she fell on her knees and began to weep.

At last she had dared come to the Master! She must have seen and heard Him several times, but never had she been so close. People like her stayed on the outskirts of the crowds that followed Him! Something in His person and words had stirred a hidden hope within her. So here she was, asking for forgiveness while her tears fell on His feet. She dried His feet with her hair, kissed them, and anointed them with oil from the costly box she had with her.

When Simon saw this he said to himself, *This Man, if He were a prophet, would have perceived who and what manner of woman this is that toucheth Him, that she is a sinner.*

Jesus turned to Simon and said, *Simon, I have somewhat to say unto thee.* He told Simon about two debtors who owed the same man different sums of money. He had forgiven them both their debts. Jesus asked Simon which one of the debtors loved the man more. Simon said, *He . . . to whom He forgave the most.*

Then said Jesus, *Seest thou this woman? I entered into thy house, thou gavest me no water for my feet: but she hath wetted my feet with tears, and wiped them with her hair. Thou gavest me no kiss: but she, since the time I came in, hath not ceased to kiss my feet. My head with oil thou didst not anoint: but she hath anointed my feet with ointment. Wherefore I say unto thee, Her sins, which are many, are forgiven; for she loved much: but to whom little is forgiven, the same loveth little.*

Jesus Forgives Mary Her Sins

Then He turned to her and said, *Thy sins are forgiven.*

The rest of the company were surprised and said within themselves, *Who is this that even forgiveth sins?* Then Jesus again spoke to the woman saying, *Thy faith hath saved thee; go in peace.*

Her stooped shoulders and bent body straightened. She arose and left the room, a forgiven woman with a new chance in life. (This story is based on Luke 7:36-50.)

LESSON TEXT

Thy sins are forgiven. Luke 7:48.

HYMN (See page 143)

PRAYER

Dear God, forgive us our sins; help us to forgive those who trespass against us; for Jesus' sake. Amen.

BIBLE STUDY

1. Beginning with Romans, look up each of the following five books. Note the name of each book.
2. Name the first five books of the New Testament.
3. Name the last five.
4. Whose story is told in each of the four Gospels?
5. Luke wrote Acts. What other book did he write? Who was he?
6. Today's story is based on Luke 7:36-50. Read it.

QUESTIONS

1. What is the Lesson Text? What did those words do to the sinful woman?
2. Why was she quiet when she came into the room? Why had she come?
3. What did she do when she came to Jesus?
4. Did Simon like what the woman did? Did Simon think that Jesus knew what sort of woman she was?
5. Did Jesus know what Simon thought? How do you know?
6. What story does Jesus tell Simon? What does Jesus want to teach Simon?
7. How does Jesus compare Simon with the sinful woman?
8. What hope did the woman have? How had she gotten it? How did she get her forgiveness? (See Third Article.)
9. What effect did Jesus' words have on her?
10. What must she do to stay a good woman?
11. Where in the Catechism do we learn about the forgiveness of sins?

Chapter 21

THE THIRD ARTICLE — OF SANCTIFICATION

I believe that . . . the Holy Spirit . . . at the last day will raise up me and all the dead, and will grant everlasting life to me and to all who believe in Christ. This is most certainly true.

Jesus Raises Jairus' Daughter

JAIRUS was one of the rulers of the synagogue in Capernaum. Many of these rulers did not believe in Jesus, but Jairus did.

Once, when his twelve-year-old daughter became very sick, Jairus went out in search of the Great Healer. He found Him with a multitude at the seaside. He knelt at Jesus feet, worshipped Him, and besought Him much saying, *My little daughter is at the point of death: I pray Thee, that Thou come and lay Thy hands on her, that she may be made whole, and live.*

Jesus at once went with him. While they were yet on the way, some people came from Jairus' house to tell him his daughter was now dead. There was no need of troubling the Teacher any further.

It was a hard blow for Jairus. After all, he had reached Jesus too late. But Jesus knew what Jairus was thinking and said, *Fear not, only believe.* When they reached the house, Jesus entered with Peter, James, and John. They found the house filled with hired mourners, as the custom was.

Jesus asked them why they were making such noise. The girl was not dead, only asleep. But they had seen death before and knew better, so they laughed at Him. Jesus told the hired mourners to leave the house, and they obeyed Him.

With the father and mother and the three disciples He went to the bedside. He took the small hand in His, and said: *Damsel, I say to thee, Arise.* She began to breathe and opened her eyes, as if waking from a deep sleep. She clung to His hand as she sat up and looked around her. Then she stepped out of her bed, a well girl. Jesus told her parents to give her something to eat. The mother at once got busy and we may be sure she put on the table the best she had.

Jesus asked them not to tell others about this miracle. We believe that they obeyed His request although it must have been

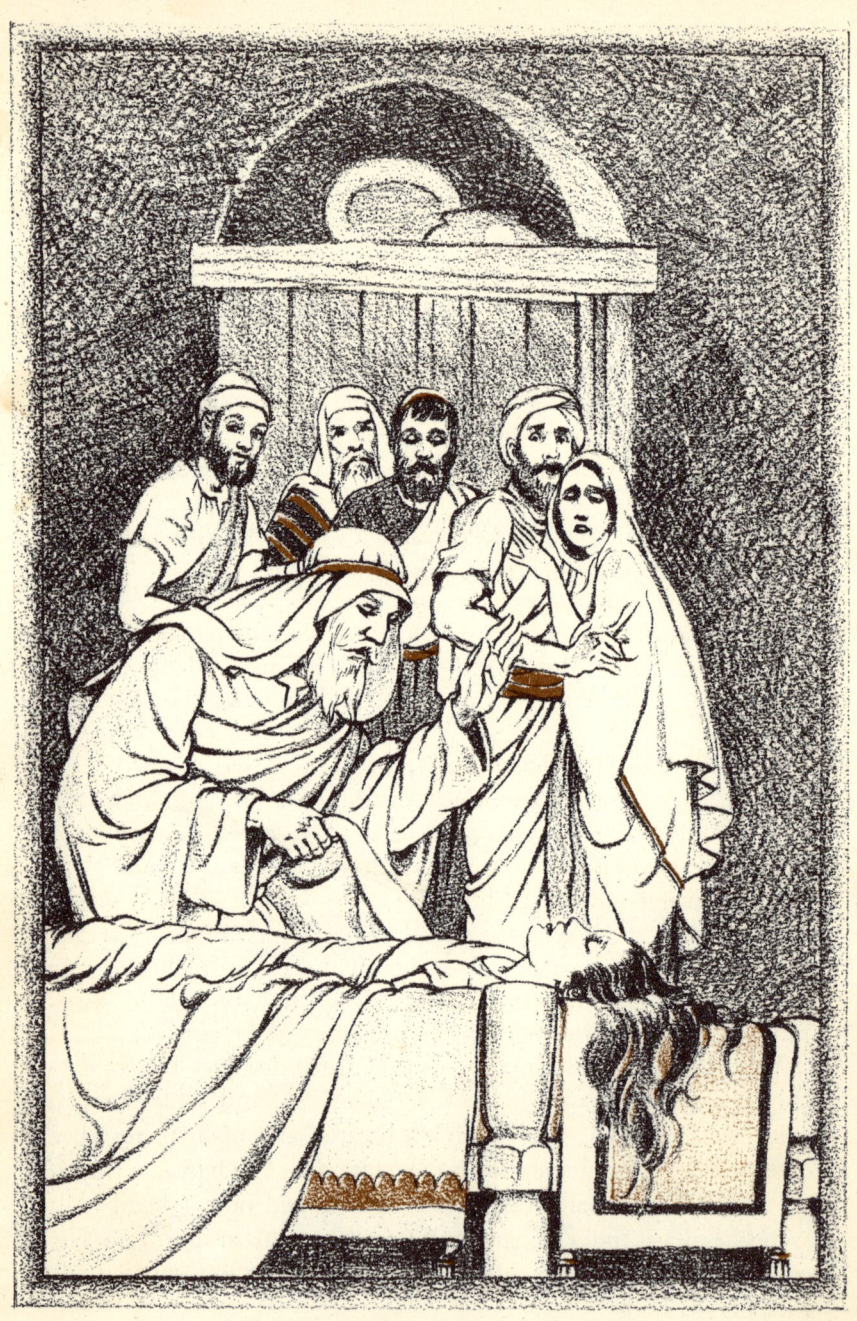
"Damsel, I say unto thee, Arise."

hard to do so. But others knew, and the news spread. Of one thing we may be certain, that those happy parents often told the girl how Jesus raised her from the dead. Nothing could shake their faith in Jesus as the Lord over life and death. (This story is based on Mark 5:21-24; 35-43.)

LESSON TEXT

Damsel, I say unto thee, Arise. Mark 5:41.

HYMN (See page 143)

PRAYER

We thank Thee, dear Lord Jesus, that Thou art the Lord of life and that Thy people shall live forever and forever. Amen.

BIBLE STUDY

1. Beginning with Romans, name the next five books.
2. Paul wrote these six books.
3. Who wrote the book of Acts?
4. What does the Book of Acts tell about?
5. To whom was the Epistle to the Hebrews written?
6. Who wrote Revelation? What other books did he write?
7. Today's story is based on Mark 5:21-24 and 35-43. Read it.

QUESTIONS

1. To whom did Jesus say the words in our Lesson Text? Why?
2. How was Jairus different from many other rulers of the synagogue?
3. Was the girl dead when the father started out to look for Jesus? How do you know? What can we learn from Jairus?
4. Why did Jairus think he had come to Jesus too late? Had he?
5. Who went with Him into the house? Can you see any reason why Jesus took them with Him inside? (Witnesses; left records for us, etc.)
6. Who told this miracle abroad although Jesus asked that it be kept quiet?
7. What will Jesus do to all His believers now sleeping in their graves?
8. When will He do this?
   The believers in God are only bodily dead; their souls are with God; on that day He will raise the bodies of all people. He will give life everlasting to all who died believing in Him and they shall live in heaven forever with Jesus.

Chapter 22

THE LORD'S PRAYER — THE INTRODUCTION

Our Father, who art in heaven.

QUESTION: What does this mean?

ANSWER: God thereby tenderly encourages us to believe that He is truly our Father, and that we are truly His children, so that we may boldly and confidently come to Him in prayer, even as beloved children come to their dear father.

Jesus in Prayer

THE evening before He died on the cross, Jesus was together with His disciples eating the Passover lamb. Let us step inside and see what is going on.

They have all taken their places at the table. They are waiting, for the dust has not been washed off their bare feet. This is a servant's duty, but there is no servant present. Not one of the disciples is willing to do the servant's work. So Jesus Himself gets up and washes the twenty-four feet.

The meal begins. While eating, Jesus institutes the Lord's Supper. He tells Judas that he is planning to betray his Lord, and with a scowling look Judas leaves the room. During the meal they sing several Old Testament Psalms. Jesus tells them that He is going to His Father and that He will send the Holy Spirit to comfort them. He tells them that death has no power over Him. He shall live and therefore they shall live also. The world will hate them, He says. Still, they should be of good cheer, for He has overcome the world.

When Jesus has finished speaking He turns to God in prayer. His first words are:

Father, the hour is come.

The next day Jesus was to die on the cross and He knew it. Still, when He begins to pray that last evening, His first word is, *Father*. He knew His Father, His love, and His faithfulness. Even on the way to the cross Jesus trusted and loved Him. So He confidently tells His Father that the bitter hour has come.

Glorify Thy Son, that the Son may glorify Thee, He says. And He adds, *I glorified Thee on earth, having accomplished the work which Thou hast given Me to do.*

Jesus Prays in the Garden of Gethsemane

Jesus asks the Father to help Him carry out His life's purpose. He could speak to God fearlessly and gladly about the work He had done. He had nothing to be ashamed of. Everything had been done as the Father wanted it done. Jesus had never sought His own honor and glory. To glorify His Father was His life's purpose. Now He asks that the Father will stand by Him the last night and day so that He just as gladly may finish the work. By His willing obedience Jesus had glorified God during His life. He asks that He may glorify God also in His bitter death.

Now Jesus begins to pray for His disciples. *I pray for them,* He says. He is happy to be able to tell the Father that they had kept the word Jesus had spoken to them. *Holy Father, keep them in Thy name,* He pleads. *I pray, not that Thou shouldest take them from the world, but that Thou shouldest keep them from the evil one.* The disciples had work to do in this world and Jesus prays that they may not fail. There is only one way in which this prayer can be fulfilled. So Jesus adds, *Sanctify them in the truth: Thy word is truth.*

Let us listen once more.

Neither for these only do I pray, but for them also that believe on Me through their word.

Jesus knew that the work of the disciples would bear fruit. The Gospel would be preached in all the world, and people without number would accept Jesus as their Lord and Savior. So Jesus prays for all believers in all countries and in all ages.

That they may all be one, He prays. He means that all believers may love and serve Him and then they will love and serve one another. (This story is based on John 17.)

LESSON TEXT

Therefore I say unto you, All things whatsoever ye pray and ask for, believe that ye receive them, and ye shall have them. Mark 11:24.

HYMN (See page 143)

PRAYER

Our Father who art in heaven;
Hallowed be Thy name;
Thy kingdom come;
Thy will be done on earth, as it is in heaven;
Give us this day our daily bread;
And forgive us our trespasses, as we forgive those who trespass against us;

And lead us not into temptation;
But deliver us from evil;
For Thine is the kingdom, and the power, and the glory, for ever and ever.
Amen.

BIBLE STUDY

1. Name the first eleven books of the New Testament.
2. Find the Epistle to the Colossians.
3. Look up the next six books. Name them.
4. These seven books were also written by Paul.
5. Paul wrote thirteen of the New Testament books.
6. Today's story is based on John 17. Find it and read it.

QUESTIONS

1. Why were none of the disciples willing to wash the feet of the others?
2. Which sacrament did Jesus institute while eating the Passover lamb?
3. How could the disciples be of good cheer going out into a world that would hate them?
4. For whom does Jesus pray first?
5. For what does He pray in this part of the prayer?
6. For whom does He pray next?
7. For what does He pray in this part of the prayer?
8. Does Jesus pray for anyone else?
9. What does He ask God to do for them?
10. For how many does Jesus pray in this last part of the prayer?

The Galatians Welcome Paul

Chapter 23

THE LORD'S PRAYER — THE FIRST PETITION

Hallowed be Thy name.

QUESTION: What does this mean?

ANSWER: God's name is indeed holy in itself; but we pray in this petition that it may be hallowed also among us.

QUESTION: How is this done?

ANSWER: When the Word of God is taught in its truth and purity and we, as God's children, lead holy lives, in accordance with it. This grant us, dear Father in heaven! But whoever teaches and lives otherwise than God's Word teaches, profanes the name of God among us. From this preserve us, heavenly Father!

Paul Fights for the Pure Gospel

THE apostle Paul made three missionary journeys. Each time he started from Antioch in Syria. It was on the second journey that he and Silas came to Galatia in Asia Minor. He stayed there for some time preaching the gospel and organizing churches.

Many of the Galatians were glad to hear the gospel. It was indeed good news that Christ had died for their sins. They had lived ungodly lives and their sins were many. Never before had they been told that the blood of Christ cleansed from all sins. They accepted Christ as their Savior and Lord and became God's happy children. Their hearts were changed and as a result they broke with their old sins and began to serve Christ. They were even persecuted for being Christians, and still they were happy.

Though Paul was not well at the time, the Galatians accepted him as an angel of God, yes, even as Christ Jesus Himself. Paul had an eye trouble that greatly weakened his sight. So warmly did they love him that they would have plucked out their own eyes and given him if it would have helped him.

After Paul had left Galatia some Jews came and told the Christians that Paul was preaching a false gospel. If they wanted to be saved they would have to believe and live as the Jews did. They must live according to the Jewish law. They must not sit down to eat with Gentiles. On the Sabbath they must not walk more than a Sabbath day's journey, about one mile. They must not eat pork or other food declared unclean by the law. And above all, they must be circumcised.

Little by little the Galatians began to listen to these false teachers and believe what they preached.

When Paul heard what was going on in the Galatian congregations he was greatly disturbed. As a rule some one wrote his letters at his dictation because of his poor eye-sight. This time he sat down and wrote a letter in his own hand. He used large letters so he could see what he wrote. This letter is the Epistle to the Galatians in our Bible.

Two times in this letter he says, that if an angel from heaven or anyone else should preach another gospel than the one he preached, that person should be accursed. He meant that he would be under God's judgment. He tells them that he had his gospel from Christ Himself. If they accepted the Jewish teaching they would have no part in Christ. There would be no salvation for them.

Why did Paul use such strong language? Because he knew that false teachings profaned the name of God. The false teachers did not tell the truth about God and His salvation. It is Christ and Christ alone that tells us the full truth about God.

There was also another thing the Galatians should remember. The false teachers wanted to win them over to their faith so they could go around and brag about it. Paul had worked to win them for Christ. He wanted to glorify Christ. The crucified Savior was no disgrace to Paul. He was his glory. *Far be it from me,* he writes, *to glory, save in the cross of our Lord Jesus Christ.* (This story is based on Galatians 1:6-10.)

LESSON TEXT

Far be it from me to glory, save in the cross of our Lord Jesus Christ. Galatians 6:14.

HYMN (See page 143)

PRAYER

Based on First Petition.

BIBLE STUDY

1. How many New Testament books did Paul write? Name them.
2. Find the Epistle of James.
3. Look up the two books following James. Name them.
4. Read Galatians 1:6-12. Also Galatians 6:11-18.

QUESTIONS

1. What does *hallow* mean? (To set apart for holy or religious use.)
2. What does Paul say about hallowing God's name? (Lesson Text.)
3. Where do we find Paul and Silas in this lesson?
4. How did the Galatians receive Paul?
5. Why did Paul continue preaching though he was ill?
6. What did he preach to the Galatians? What did the Jewish teachers preach? Can you tell exactly how Paul's teaching differed from theirs? (See Galatians 6:14-15.)
7. What did the Jewish teachers say about Paul?
8. From whom did Paul receive his gospel? (Galatians 1:12.)
9. What was Paul's purpose in preaching the gospel?
10. Why did Paul use such strong language in this letter?
11. Explain how this lesson illustrates the First Petition.

Paul Preaches to the Galatians

Chapter 24

THE LORD'S PRAYER — THE SECOND PETITION

Thy kingdom come.

QUESTION: What does this mean?

ANSWER: The kingdom of God comes indeed of itself, without our prayer; but we pray in this petition that it may come also to us.

QUESTION: How is this done?

ANSWER: When our heavenly Father gives us His Holy Spirit, so that by His grace we believe His holy Word, and live a godly life here on earth, and in heaven for ever.

Paul and the Philippians

PAUL was on his second missionary journey. In Troas a man came to him in a dream saying, *Come over into Macedonia and help us.* The day after the vision Paul set sail across the Ægean Sea. He landed in Macedonia in Europe, and went to Philippi.

It was a heathen city located in a gold-mining region. Roman soldiers were there to enforce the law because it was a Roman colony. They were rough and harsh. They used the most cruel way to govern. Often this was needed because adventurers, gamblers, and crooks of every kind came here to make easy money.

Money was the thing everyone was after. The desire for it led men and women, young and old, into gross sins: theft, murder, adultery, and every known vice. Homes were broken up, and children set adrift. The owners were cruel to the slaves who did all the work. The rich brow-beat the poor, the soldiers tortured their prisoners, and so on in endless line.

Might was right. The rich wallowed in ease and plenty while the poor suffered in squalor and want. But rich or poor, they enjoyed themselves in whatever wickedness they could afford.

Into such a place Paul came to preach. He set to work with prayer in his heart. The people were hard to reach. Besides being wicked they were also proud. They thought of themselves as Roman citizens: rich, powerful, well-governed, belonging to the mightiest nation in the world. But Paul made a beginning. Fearlessly he told them of their sins and their need of a Savior.

The first to listen and become a Christian was Lydia, a seller

Paul Baptizes the Jailer

of purple. The second one to accept Christ was a slave girl. Paul rid her of her evil fortune-telling spirit. Her owners complained because without that spirit she could earn no money for them. Paul was beaten and thrown into jail. That night Paul baptized the jailer and his household into the new church. In this way the church at Philippi started with just a few believers.

A miracle came about. The gospel spread and opened the eyes of the Philippians to their sins. They saw their need of Christ and accepted Him as their Savior and Lord. They became humble, helpful, clean, praying people. They were eager to carry on the missionary work that had brought salvation to them. They also sent help to other churches.

Later when Paul was in prison in Rome the Philippians sent a messenger to him with a gift. Usually he did not accept gifts from the churches because he did not want to give anyone the chance to say that he preached Christ for the sake of money. But Paul had such a confidence in the Philippians that he took their gift and wrote a letter of thanks to them, not for the gift alone, but for their share in spreading the gospel. This letter is called Paul's Letter to the Philippians and is in the New Testament.

This is the story of the church at Philippi, the first Christian church in Europe. (This story is based on the Epistle to the Philippians.)

LESSON TEXT

Fear not, little flock; for it is your Father's good pleasure to give you the kingdom. Luke 12:32.

HYMN (See page 143)

PRAYER

We thank Thee, Lord Jesus, that Thy Word has come to us. Help us to believe and obey it and to spread it to others. Amen.

BIBLE STUDY

1. Beginning with Hebrews, name the books to the end of the Bible.
2. Name the first five books of the New Testament.
3. Name the books written by Paul.
4. Read Philippians 1:1-11.
5. How did Paul feel towards the Philippians? Prove it from what you read.

QUESTIONS

1. What is the Second Petition? What is meant by this?
2. To whom did the kingdom in our lesson come? How did it come to them?
3. What kind of people were the Philippians when Paul first came to them?
4. Why did Paul go to them? How did he set about his missionary work?
5. How was he treated? Why was he put in prison? What did he do while there?
6. What did the Philippians do after they became Christians?
7. How did they show they had changed toward Paul?
8. How does Paul show that he trusts them?
9. Why does he thank God upon all his remembrance of them?
10. Why are they an example of God's kingdom come on earth?

Paul on the Road to Damascus

Chapter 25

THE LORD'S PRAYER — THE THIRD PETITION

Thy will be done on earth, as it is in heaven.

QUESTION: What does this mean?

ANSWER: The good and gracious will of God is done indeed without our prayer; but we pray in this petition that it may be done also among us.

QUESTION: How is this done?

ANSWER: When God destroys and brings to naught every evil counsel and purpose of the devil, the world, and our own flesh, which would hinder us from hallowing His name, and prevent the coming of His kingdom; and when He strengthens us and keeps us steadfast in His Word and in faith, even unto our end. This is His good and gracious will.

Paul, the Sufferer for Christ

BEFORE Paul became a Christian he was called Saul. He was a strict Jew. He believed that Christ was a false prophet who would destroy the religion of Israel. He hated the Christians and their Christ. He persecuted all Jews who became Christians in order to force them to deny Christ. It was not enough for him to persecute the Christians in Jerusalem. When he heard that many Jews in Damascus had accepted Christ he decided to punish them, too. For that reason he was now on his way to Damascus to destroy the church there.

But it was not to be as he planned. On the way he met Christ in a vision. Christ asked him, *Why persecutest thou Me?* Paul asked in return, *Who art Thou, Lord?* Christ answered, *I am Jesus whom thou persecutest.* Paul was struck with blindness and for three days he could not see, eat, or drink. He was sick with grief and sorrow because he had persecuted the Lord Jesus.

God sent a Christian by the name of Ananias to him. He came and talked to him about Christ, and baptized him into the Christian church. Ananias told him that Christ wanted him to be His witness before kings and nations, and that in this work he would have to go through many sufferings. Paul promised Christ that he would serve Him no matter what it might cost him. From the moment he began to preach he suffered all and even more than he had made the Christians suffer.

The Jews tried to kill him. In speaking of his sufferings Paul says in II Corinthians 11:24-28, *Of the Jews five times received I forty stripes save one. Thrice was I beaten with rods, once was I stoned, thrice I suffered shipwreck, a night and a day have I been in the deep; ... in labor and travail, in watchings often, in hunger and thirst, in fastings often, in cold and nakedness.*

Again and again he was arrested, tortured, and imprisoned. Once he was held prisoner in his own hired house for two years. But even then he worked for Christ. After he became a Christian he had only one purpose. He wanted to serve and glorify

Paul Sends a Letter from Prison

Christ. It was Christ alone that ruled his life. Paul said, *For to me to live is Christ.* (This story is based on Acts 9:1-19.)

LESSON TEXT

He that loseth his life for My sake shall find it. Matthew 10:39.

HYMN (See page 143)

PRAYER

My God and Father, help me always to pray: Thy will be done on earth, as it is in heaven. Amen.

BIBLE STUDY

1. Name all New Testament books in their order.
2. Name the books written by (A) Luke, (B) John, (C) Paul.
3. What books did Peter write?
4. Between what two books do you find the Epistle of Jude?
5. Between what two books do you find Hebrews?
6. Read II Corinthians 11:24-28.

QUESTIONS

1. What did Paul believe about Jesus before he was converted?
2. Why did he think as he did? How did he treat the Christians? Why?
3. How did he find out his mistake about Jesus?
4. What was God's will with Paul? (Bible References, Colossians 1:24-25 and Acts 9:15-16.)
5. Where did he get strength to do God's will? (His Word—see Catechism.)
6. Who tried to keep him from doing God's will? How? Why did they not succeed? (God hindered them—see Catechism.)
7. Prove that Paul's sufferings did not take away the joy and peace he had in Christ. (Bible Reference, Colossians 1:24-25; also the story.)

Paul Taken to Prison

Chapter 26

THE LORD'S PRAYER — THE FOURTH PETITION

Give us this day our daily bread.

QUESTION: What does this mean?

ANSWER: God indeed gives daily bread to all men, even to the wicked, without our prayer; but we pray in this petition that He would lead us to acknowledge our daily bread as His gift, and to receive it with thanksgiving.

QUESTION: What is meant by daily bread?

ANSWER: Everything that is required to satisfy our bodily needs; such as food and raiment, house and home, fields and flocks, money and goods; pious parents, children, and servants; godly and faithful rulers, good government; seasonable weather, peace and health; order and honor; true friends, good neighbors, and the like.

Paul the Missionary

PAUL was born of Jewish parents in Tarsus, a school town in southern Cilica. His father was a Roman citizen, an honor seldom given a Jew. From his earliest childhood Paul learned his nation's history, religion, and hopes of a coming Messiah. His parents planned that he should be a rabbi. As Paul grew up he learned three things: the Jewish religion; Greek books and art; and an understanding of Roman government.

These advantages (though they at first helped him in his fight against Christ, Chapter 25) prepared him for his missionary work. He also had another help in the work. His parents in training him to be a rabbi had taught him how to make tents. Every rabbi had to have a trade.

At that time there was no church, mission society, or other organization to support a missionary. Paul had to earn his living by making tents. In the Jewish colonies he found work every where, and a ready sale for his tents. In Corinth he lived at the home of Aquila and Priscilla. They too worked at tent-making. During the day Paul was busy weaving and sewing tents. In the evenings and on the Sabbath he would go where the people came together and preach the gospel.

Paul Makes Tents

Though Paul could use only part of his time for preaching and teaching, this did not hinder his work for Christ. Because he could make his living anywhere he was free to come and go as the Holy Spirit led him.

His tent-making was also a way of preaching the Gospel. With the exception of the Jews, people looked upon manual labor as fit only for slaves. By working with his hands Paul taught the people that work was not a shame. It is God's will that man should work.

Paul was a missionary for Christ when he preached and when he made tents. (This story is based on Acts 18:1-7.)

LESSON TEXT

The Lord is my shepherd; I shall not want. Psalm 23:1.

HYMN (See page 143)

PRAYER

Teach class to sing No. 568, v. 1 in Lutheran Hymnary.

Great God, we praise Thy gracious care,
Which does our daily bread prepare;
O bless the earthly food we take,
And feed our souls for Jesus' sake. Amen.

BIBLE STUDY

1. Name the first five books in the Bible.
2. Name the five books written by the Major Prophets.
3. Find the Book of Nehemiah.
4. What book comes before Nehemiah? And after?
5. Read II Thessalonians 3:10. Memorize this verse.
6. Read Acts 18:1-7.

QUESTIONS

1. Who was Paul? What four things did he learn as he grew up?
2. How did he happen to learn each of the four things?
3. His faith and trade helped him most in his work for Christ. Why?
4. Why did Paul work at his trade while preaching? You will find three reasons in the story.
5. With whom did he stay in Corinth? Why?
6. When did Paul do his preaching? Do you think he did any missionary work while he sat at his tent-making?
7. Why need we not worry about our daily bread? (Lesson Text.)
8. Show that the Hymn can be said of Paul.

Chapter 27
THE LORD'S PRAYER — THE FIFTH PETITION

And forgive us our trespasses, as we forgive those who trespass against us.

QUESTION: What does this mean?

ANSWER: We pray in this petition that our heavenly Father would not regard our sins nor because of them deny our prayers; for we neither merit nor are worthy of those things for which we pray; but that He would grant us all things through grace, even though we sin daily, and deserve nothing but punishment. And certainly we, on our part, will heartily forgive, and gladly do good to those who may sin against us.

Stephen, the First Christian Martyr

THE Christians chose Stephen to be one of the seven deacons of the new church in Jerusalem. It was the duty of the deacons to give out food and clothing to the needy Christians.

Stephen was filled with the power of God to heal the sick and do many other miracles. He was also a powerful preacher. He told the Jews that Jesus was the promised Savior who was to bring to an end the sacrifices and the services of the temple. Jesus meant so much to him that he had to tell everybody about Him.

The leaders were seriously troubled. They felt that they had to put a stop to this preaching. To begin with they tried to show that Stephen was wrong. He did not understand the Old Testament, they claimed. But Stephen understood God's plan with His people better than the leaders did.

Still, they would not give in. They bribed false witnesses to testify that Stephen had spoken evil against Moses and against

The Stoning of Stephen

God. He was brought before the council for a hearing. The false witnesses again testified against him. They said that Stephen had preached that Jesus would destroy the temple and change the teachings of Moses.

All eyes in the council were fastened on Stephen and they saw his face shining as if it had been the face of an angel. Jesus was with His servant, giving him strength and joy to bear witness of his Lord and Savior.

Then Stephen said to them, "You are stiff-necked and always resist the Holy Spirit. Your fathers persecuted the prophets and killed them that foretold the coming of Christ and you have betrayed and murdered Him."

The council and all present became so angry that they gnashed their teeth at Stephen. But he looked steadfastly into heaven and said, *Behold, I see the heavens opened, and the Son of Man standing at the right hand of God.* A shout of anger filled the room. They rushed at Stephen and dragged him out of the city.

When they came to a suitable place they formed a circle around him. They took off their outer garments and laid them at the feet of a young man by the name of Saul. Then the stone-throwing began. The stones came thick and fast and Stephen soon felt that the end was coming. He called upon the Lord and said, *Lord Jesus, receive my spirit.* Then he knelt down and cried with a loud voice, *Lord, lay not this sin to their charge.* And when he had said this he fell asleep.

Thus died the first Christian martyr, praying that the Lord Jesus would forgive those who killed him. (This story is based on Acts 6 and 7.)

LESSON TEXT
Lord, lay not this sin to their charge. Acts 7:60.

HYMN (See page 143)

PRAYER
"And forgive us our trespasses, as we forgive those who trespass against us." Amen.

BIBLE STUDY
1. Name the first fourteen books of the Bible.
2. Name the three books between II Chronicles and Job.
3. Look up the three books between Psalms and Isaiah. Name them. Together with Job and Psalms they are called the poetical books.
4. Read Acts 7:54-60.

QUESTIONS

1. When did Stephen pray the words of our Lesson Text?
2. Who was Stephen? Why did people feel his power?
3. What two things did Stephen do for the people?
4. Who tried to argue with him? Why? Why did they get angry with Stephen?
5. How did his enemies win against him? What commandment did they break?
6. Of what did Stephen accuse the leaders? Prove that he spoke the truth about them.
7. What did the leaders do when Stephen pointed out their sins to them?
8. What did Stephen see that encouraged him? (See Acts 6:7.)
9. What two prayers did he pray? Which one do most of us forget?
10. What do you think Stephen saw as he knelt the last time?
11. How is Stephen's prayer for his enemies like Jesus' prayer on the Cross? (See Luke 23:34.)
12. Of what was Stephen accused? Christ was accused of the same thing. (See Matthew 26:65.)
13. Stephen's vision of the Son of man is the same as spoken of in Matthew 26:64. Find it; read what Jesus says about the Son of man.
14. How did Stephen feel toward those who killed him? What did he do for them?

Chapter 28

THE LORD'S PRAYER — THE SIXTH PETITION

And lead us not into temptation.

QUESTION: What does this mean?

ANSWER: God indeed tempts no one to sin; but we pray in this petition that God would so guard and preserve us, that the devil, the world, and our own flesh may not deceive us, nor lead us into error and unbelief, despair, and other great and shameful sins; but that, when so tempted, we may finally prevail and gain the victory.

Judas Betrays Jesus

JUDAS ISCARIOT was one of the twelve disciples. He was their treasurer, too. He knew that the leaders of the people in Jerusalem, especially the scribes and the Pharisees, were looking for a chance to arrest Jesus. They dared not do it openly because they were afraid of the people. Judas felt sure that they would pay for any help that he might give them. The more he thought of the money Jesus might bring him the more he wanted it. At last he could not look at Jesus without wondering what price the enemies would give for Him.

One day he went to the chief priests and asked what they would pay for Jesus. They gave him thirty pieces of silver. From that time Judas was on the lookout for a chance to betray Jesus into their hands. The other disciples knew nothing about the shameful scheme of Judas. How did he dare to sit with the others at the Passover feast with the thirty pieces in his purse? When Jesus said that one of them would betray Him, Judas looked as surprised as the rest.

While they were eating, Jesus dipped the sop, gave it to Judas and said, *What thou doest, do quickly.* Then Judas yielded completely to Satan. He went out into the night.

He hurried to the high priests and told them everything was ready. Then he led the officers from the chief priests, the soldiers, and others to the garden of Gethsemane.

Jesus saw them coming. Their weapons glittered in the light

Judas Betrays Jesus

of the lanterns and torches. Judas led the way. He came to Jesus and said, *Hail, Rabbi,* and bent forward and kissed Him. That was the sign by which the soldiers were to know Jesus.

Jesus looked with sorrow at His betrayer and said, *Judas, betrayest thou the Son of man with a kiss?*

When Jesus was sentenced to die it seemed to shock Judas. He saw how dreadfully he had sinned. He had not listened to his conscience, but now he could not stop its accusations. Why had he done this thing? Why had he not repented and confessed? Jesus had tried to save him. Now it was too late. He had sold his best Friend for thirty pieces of silver. He could not bear the terrible thought. He found a rope and hanged himself. (This story is based on Matthew 26:47-50.)

LESSON TEXT

For what doth it profit a man, to gain the whole world, and forfeit his life? Mark 8:36.

HYMN (See page 143)

PRAYER

God and Father, when Satan tempts me help me to listen to Thy voice in my conscience. Help me to pray and to obey Thee. Keep me and give me victory. Amen.

BIBLE STUDY

1. Name the poetical books in the Bible.
2. Name the first three of the Minor Prophets. Look up these three books.
3. What is the next to the last book in the Old Testament?
4. What book comes before it and after it?
5. Read Matthew 26:47-50.

QUESTIONS

1. Who was Judas? How did he know the leaders wanted to arrest Jesus? (Read John 5:18.)
2. Why did Judas want to betray his Savior?
3. Did the other disciples know what Judas was planning to do?
4. Why did Judas understand Jesus when he said, "What thou doest, do quickly," and the other disciples did not? What did the others think Jesus meant? (Read John 13:27-29.)
5. Why did Jesus say that to Judas?
6. Did Jesus try to give Judas a chance to repent? When?
7. Was Judas sorry for what he had done? If so, why was he not saved?
8. Do you think Jesus was ready to help him?
9. What could Judas have done to be true to Jesus? (Catechism Text.)

Chapter 29

THE LORD'S PRAYER — THE SEVENTH PETITION

But deliver us from evil.

QUESTION: What does this mean?

ANSWER: We pray in this petition, as in a summary, that our heavenly Father would deliver us from all manner of evil, whether it affect body or soul, property or reputation, and at last, when the hour of death shall come, grant us a blessed end, and graciously take us from this world of sorrow to Himself in heaven.

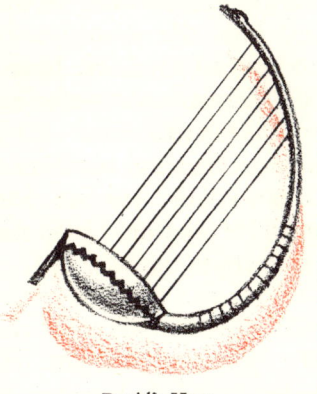

David's Harp

Saul Pursues David

WHEN Saul became the first king of Israel (Chapter 8) Samuel hoped he would serve God, but time and again Saul disobeyed God and went his own way. Samuel warned him that God would choose another man to be king over His people. Although Saul was afraid of losing his throne, he would not obey God. His guilty conscience made him worse day by day. An evil spirit came upon him and filled him with fear, anger, hatred, and jealousy. At last he was no longer the same man Samuel had anointed to be king of Israel.

The Philistines were again raiding the land of Israel as they had done many times before. In their army was a giant, Goliath. He sneered and mocked Saul's army. He dared them to send a man to fight him. So far no one had taken the dare.

One day young David came with food for his brothers in the army. When he heard of Goliath he said he would fight him. He took his sling and some smooth stones and went out against the giant. He placed a stone in the sling, whirled it, and hit Goliath so that he fell. Then he rushed to him, killed him and brought the giant's head to Saul.

Saul liked young David and made him leader of a hundred men in the army. When they returned from the battle, some women met them with music and singing. They sang gaily one to another. *Saul hath slain his thousands, and David his ten thousands.* This made Saul so jealous and angry that from that day he tried to kill the young hero.

One day David stood before the king playing the harp as was his duty. From his chair Saul watched him. He seemed to be listening to the music, but suddenly his arm stiffened. He leaned forward, and sent his spear flying to pin David to the wall. But the young player jumped aside and was not hurt.

This happened again that day and once later on, but David, who had learned to understand Saul, was on the lookout. The jealousy of the king became more violent every time David did anything that made the people love and praise him.

Finally, in order to be safe, David had to flee into the mountains with some of his followers. He lived first in one cave and then in another to keep away from the spies Saul sent out. He seldom asked anyone for help because the king killed anyone he found helping David.

How insane Saul was is shown by the fact that he was ready to kill his son, Jonathan, who had helped David get away. Saul

David Refuses to Kill Saul

needed every extra man and the whole army to fight the enemy; and yet he wasted time and men in chasing David who was ready to help him. Even while a fugitive, David used his men against the Philistines whenever he had the chance.

Many a time when Saul was after him, David had the chance to kill him. His men urged him to do it. They said that God placed the king in such places just for that purpose; but David would not harm the Lord's anointed. He trusted God to take care of him and deliver him from all evil. And God did keep him and make him king over Israel. (This story is based on I Samuel 18:6-9.)

LESSON TEXT

I will fear no evil; for Thou art with me. Psalm 23:4.

HYMN (See page 144)

PRAYER

"Help me, O Lord my God;
Oh save me according to Thy lovingkindness." Psalm 109:26

BIBLE STUDY

1. Name the first three and the last three books of the Minor Prophets.
2. Find the Book of Jonah.
3. What book comes before it and what book comes after it?
4. Name the books between Ruth and Job.
5. Memorize Psalm 23. It is called the Shepherd Psalm.

QUESTIONS

1. Why did Saul hate David?
2. When did he first try to kill David? How?
3. What did David do after that?
4. Why was it easy for Saul to know where David was?
5. Why did not God remove the danger from David?
6. How could David have destroyed Saul? Why did he not do it?
7. Why was David safe in spite of danger? (Lesson Text.)
8. Show that the Seventh Petition and the Prayer verse mean the same.

Chapter 30

THE LORD'S PRAYER — THE CONCLUSION

For Thine is the kingdom, and the power, and the glory, for ever and ever. Amen.

QUESTION: What does the word "Amen" mean?

ANSWER: It means that I should be assured that such petitions are acceptable to our heavenly Father, and are heard by Him; for He Himself has commanded us to pray in this manner, and has promised to hear us. Amen, Amen, that is, Yea, yea, it shall be so.

God Answers Moses

MOSES called the Israelites to a stop at Rephidim. He was sad because his people murmured and doubted God every time something went wrong with them. The journey from Egypt to the promised land had been full of danger, but God had helped them on the way. Their wanderings in the wilderness now were hard. They seemed to be tired and thirsty most of the time. Moses knew it was best to stop for rest and for prayer.

As the Israelites neared Mount Sinai, Amalek was ready to attack them. Amalek was king of the nomadic tribe north of Rephidim. Moses was surprised when the runners came with news of the attack. As the news spread, the people became panic-stricken. It was not easy to quiet some two million frightened people. Moses saw that it would be necessary to drive the enemy away. He therefore said to Joshua, *Choose us out men and go out, fight with Amalek*. Moses himself with Aaron and Hur went up on a hill to pray God for help and victory.

God could have destroyed the enemy even if the Israelites had not fought. He did so at the Red Sea when He destroyed the Egyptians. However, it was needed to build up courage and manhood in His chosen people, the Israelites. For this reason they had to learn to defend themselves. They also had to learn another truth. Even though they knew how to defend themselves, victory would depend upon God's help.

As was the custom among them, Moses stretched his arms toward heaven while he prayed. He held the rod of God in his hands. As long as the staff of God was uplifted in his hands

Aaron and Hur Hold Up Moses' Arms

the men of Israel won. But Moses grew tired, and his aching arms dropped. Then Israel began to lose. He knew he must hold the sign of God's help on high, but how?

A stone was brought for Moses to sit down on. Aaron and Hur stood on either side of him, and held up his tired arms while he prayed. Then the enemy lost ground and at last left the battlefield. God's people were saved. His power prevailed, and to Him belonged the glory.

God told Moses to write an account of this in a book to be given to Joshua. He was to be the next leader of Israel, and should let coming generations know that all power and glory belong to God. (This story is based on Exodus 17:8-16.)

LESSON TEXT

In every thing by prayer ... with thanksgiving let your requests be made known unto God. Philippians 4:6.

HYMN (See page 144)

PRAYER

The one Jesus taught us: The Lord's Prayer, the one finished in our lesson today.

BIBLE STUDY

1. Name the first six and the last three books of the Minor Prophets.
2. Find the Book of Nahum.
3. Look up and name the two books that come after Nahum.
4. Make a list of the Minor Prophets.
5. The Beatitudes are in the beginning of Matthew 5. Look up and read.
6. The Sermon on the Mount is in Matthew 5, 6, and 7. Find it.
7. Read Exodus 17:8-16.

QUESTIONS

1. Where were the Israelites going? Where were they in this lesson?
2. Who was their leader? What kind of leader was he?
3. Why did he call a stop at Rephidim?
4. Who was Amalek? What did he do?
5. Why did Moses' prayer help?
6. Who gave the victory to Israel? Why?
7. Why did not God let them win without a fight?
8. Why did God ask Moses to write an account of this battle?

   Remember that God talks to us just as He did to His people in Old Testament times. You know what to do and what not to do. How? (By the Word of God and by your conscience.)

Chapter 31
THE SACRAMENT OF BAPTISM

I

QUESTION: What is Baptism?

ANSWER: Baptism is not simply water, but it is the water used according to God's command and connected with God's word.

QUESTION: What is this word of God?

ANSWER: It is the word of our Lord Jesus Christ, as recorded in the last chapter of Matthew: "Go ye therefore, and make disciples of all the nations, baptizing them into the Name of the Father and of the Son and of the Holy Spirit."

II

QUESTION: What gifts or benefits does Baptism bestow?

ANSWER: It works forgiveness of sins, delivers from death and the devil, and gives everlasting salvation to all who believe, as the word and promise of God declare.

QUESTION: What is this word and promise of God?

ANSWER: It is the word of our Lord Jesus Christ, as recorded in the last chapter of Mark: "He that believeth and is baptized shall be saved; but he that disbelieveth shall be condemned."

Jesus Institutes Baptism

JESUS met with His disciples on a mountain in Galilee. Soon His earthly mission would be over and it would rest upon His disciples to carry on His work of spreading His kingdom on earth. He wanted them to get His vision of that kingdom as God had planned it for all people. The disciples must see the glory of being His workers and also the greatness of the work. They must teach other disciples to carry on the work after them. His work should never stop.

He looked at them lovingly as they rose from their places at His feet where they had knelt to worship Him when they came into His holy presence. When they all settled to listen to Him, He gave them the great mission command, saying:

Jesus Gives the Great Mission Command

All authority hath been given unto Me in heaven and on earth. Go ye therefore, and make disciples of all the nations, baptizing them into the name of the Father and of the Son and of the Holy Spirit: teaching them to observe all things whatsoever I commanded you: and lo, I am with you always, even unto the end of the world.

They understood the Master. He would be with them and help them to build His kingdom on earth by baptizing and teaching.

After the ascension the disciples waited in Jerusalem for the Holy Spirit as Christ had told them to do. When the Spirit had come they went out to preach and baptize. At first they preached to the grown-ups and baptized them, but as soon as the parents came to Christ their children, too, were baptized. This was what Christ wanted. He had told them to baptize and then to teach.

In that way, through infant Baptism, children are brought into the kingdom before they are old enough to be taught God's Word. They are brought into fellowship with God, and are born again by the Spirit. They do not have to wait until they are old enough to understand the things of God before they can come into His fellowship.

Baptism takes away our sins and brings us to God. It gives us everlasting life if we believe the words and promises of God. You will find these promises in Mark 16:16 and in the Catechism under "Benefits of Baptism." Jesus made these promises when He instituted Holy Baptism. (This story is based on Matthew 28:16-20.)

LESSON TEXT

And lo, I am with you always, even unto the end of the world. Matthew 28:20.

HYMN (See page 144)

PRAYER

I thank Thee, dear God and Father, that I became Thy child in baptism. Help me to live as Thy child. Amen.

BIBLE STUDY

1. Name the books of the Minor Prophets.
2. There are 39 books in the Old Testament. Can you name them?
3. Where do you find the Beatitudes?

4. Where do you find the Sermon on the Mount?
5. The Lord's Prayer is in Matthew 6:9-13. Look it up.
6. I Corinthians 13 is called the love chapter. Read it.

QUESTIONS

1. Where did Jesus meet with His disciples?
2. Why did He institute Baptism? (To save us and to keep us in His kingdom.)
3. How did He institute Baptism? (He gave His disciples the great mission command. Learn it as it is given in Jesus' words.)
4. What two things did He command the disciples to do? Which did He place first?
5. Why did He command them to baptize before they taught?
6. What is Baptism?
7. What does Baptism give us?
8. Why is infant Baptism necessary?
9. How can infants believe? (The Holy Spirit through Baptism creates faith.)
10. What does God promise all who believe and are baptized?
11. What does Jesus say about bringing children to Him? (Mark 10:14.)
12. For how long has Jesus promised to be with His disciples? (Lesson Text, Matthew 28:20.)
13. How does Baptism build up God's kingdom on earth? (By making disciples of all who believe and are baptized.)

Chapter 32
THE SACRAMENT OF BAPTISM

III

QUESTION: How can water do such great things?

ANSWER: It is not the water, indeed, that does such great things, but the word of God, connected with the water, and our faith which relies on that word of God. For without the word of God, it is simply water and no baptism. But when connected with the word of God, it is a baptism, that is, a gracious water of life and a washing of regeneration in the Holy Spirit, as St. Paul says to Titus, in the third chapter: "According to His mercy He saved us, through the washing of regeneration and renewing of the Holy Spirit, which He poured out upon us richly, through Jesus Christ our Savior; that, being justified by His grace, we might be made heirs according to the hope of eternal life. This is a faithful saying."

Cornelius Is Baptized

CORNELIUS was commander of a hundred men in the Italian division of the Roman army at Cæsarea. He was a pious man and

The Vision of Cornelius

Cornelius Welcomes Peter

worshipped the God of Israel, but as yet he had not joined the Jewish church. He taught his entire household to believe in God. He gave much to the poor and always prayed to God. But he was not sure that God had accepted him as a true worshipper. It worried him.

One day while praying he had a vision. The vision settled the question that worried him. When the angel spoke his name, Cornelius could only stare at him in fright and stammer, *What is it, Lord?* The angel answered, *Thy prayers and thine alms are gone up for a memorial before God. And now send men to Joppa, and fetch one Simon, who is surnamed Peter.*

When the angel left, Cornelius sent two of his servants and one devout soldier to get Peter. He could hardly wait for their return because he was so eager to hear what Peter had to tell him.

After four long days of waiting, Cornelius saw Peter coming and hurried to meet him. He fell down at the apostle's feet and worshipped him. Peter said, *Stand up; I myself also am a man.* The humble man arose, much surprised. Never had he been thought as good as a Jew. They talked eagerly, like old friends, as they entered the house. Here were many relatives and friends that Cornelius had invited to hear what Peter had to say.

Cornelius explained why he had sent for Peter. He asked Peter to give them God's message. Then Peter told them about Jesus and His teachings. He ended by saying, *Through His name every one that believeth on Him shall receive remission of sins.*

While Peter was still talking, they all began speaking with tongues. They praised the Lord in different languages. The Holy Spirit had given them the miraculous gift of speaking with tongues in order to prove that these Gentiles now were ready for baptism. Cornelius, too, joined in the praises. Now he understood the way of salvation. To be saved meant to trust in Christ alone and had nothing to do with his joining the Jewish church and living like a Jew. No longer did he need to sigh, weep, or be worried. Instead he praised God, moved by the Holy Spirit.

It was clear that since the Spirit had come upon Gentile as well as Jew, salvation was for all who believed in Christ. Peter commanded them to be baptized. Cornelius and his family were baptized, and received forgiveness of their sins. (This story is based on Acts 10.)

LESSON TEXT

He that believeth and is baptized shall be saved. Mark 16:16.

HYMN (See page 143)

PRAYER

Dear God, help me to grow up as a clean, strong Christian, a true disciple of Jesus Christ. Amen.

BIBLE STUDY

1. There are 27 books in the New Testament. Name them.
2. What chapter is called the love chapter?
3. Where do you find the Sermon on the Mount? The Lord's Prayer?

QUESTIONS

1. Who was Cornelius?
2. What sort of man was he? What worried him?
3. What was the Jewish belief about salvation? Why did Cornelius send for Peter?
4. What did Cornelius do while he waited for Peter to come?
5. What did he do when Peter came? What did Peter do? What did Peter mean when he said, "I myself also am a man"?
6. What did Peter do when he came into Cornelius' house?
7. What did Cornelius learn from Peter? (Lesson Text, Mark 16:16.)
8. How did Cornelius feel when he learned how to be saved?
9. How did the Spirit bear witness that they were ready to be baptized?
10. What did they receive through Baptism?
11. How can water work such great things? What does Baptism with water mean?

Chapter 33
THE SACRAMENT OF BAPTISM
IV

QUESTION: What does such baptizing with water signify?

ANSWER: It signifies that the old Adam in us, together with all sins and evil lusts, should be drowned by daily sorrow and repentance, and be put to death; and that the new man should daily come forth and rise, to live before God in righteousness and holiness for ever.

QUESTION: Where is it so written?

ANSWER: St. Paul, in the sixth chapter of the Epistle to the Romans, says: "We were buried therefore with him through baptism into death: that like as Christ was raised from the dead through the glory of the Father, so we also might walk in newness of life."

Paul Fighting the Good Fight

PAUL was a real Christian, faithful and true. *I will show him how many things he must suffer for My name's sake,* Christ had said when He called him. Paul's life was not to be an easy one.

As soon as he began to preach Jesus Christ, he was persecuted. The Jewish leaders hated him because he taught that He whom they had crucified was their Messiah.

The Gentiles hated him because he preached against their ungodly living and because he said that God would destroy idolatry. If that happened it would hurt the business of those that made and sold idols. It would also hurt others that made money on the superstitious and sinful life of the people.

Therefore, both Jews and Gentiles persecuted Paul. Time and again he was beaten, flogged, stoned, imprisoned, and driven from his place of work.

Now, Paul was no coward. He did not flee from a place in order to escape sufferings or even to save his life. He left because for the time being he could do no more for the gospel. He knew that he would be treated the same way in other places.

Still, he could not give up preaching. Christ had called him to this work, and he could not fail. A steward must be faithful, he said.

The difficulties of the churches he had founded were always on his mind. There were many enemies trying to ruin the new congregations. We have seen that the Jews worked to lead the Christians in Galatia away from the pure gospel (Chapter 23). At Corinth, pride, quarrels, and drunkenness came into the church. In almost every church there was some trouble. Paul heard about all of these things. He wrote, *There is that which presseth upon me daily, anxiety for all the churches.* When he could not go to a place himself, he wrote letters to the people or sent someone to them and prayed for them.

The Prophet Warns Paul

Paul had other troubles. He had a sinful nature, just as the rest of us have. He had to fight temptations to pride, impatience, unbelief, and many other sins. About this he wrote, *I buffet my body, and bring it into bondage: lest by any means, after that I have preached to others, I myself should be rejected.*

One day he was on his way with gifts from his churches to the mother church at Jerusalem. When he came to Cæsarea he was told by a prophet that the Jews at Jerusalem would bind him and turn him over to the Gentiles as a prisoner. The brethren pleaded with him not to go; but Paul answered, *I am ready not to be bound only, but also to die at Jerusalem for the name of the Lord Jesus.* And he went. He was brought to Rome as a prisoner, and at last he was killed for preaching Christ Jesus.

Thus the great apostle fought the good fight. When he saw that the end was near he wrote, *I have fought the good fight, I have finished the course, I have kept the faith.* (This story is based on II Corinthians 11:23-33; I Corinthians 9:27; II Timothy 4:7.)

LESSON TEXT

As therefore ye have received Christ Jesus the Lord, so walk in Him. Colossians 2:6.

HYMN (See page 144)

PRAYER

Based on Lesson Text.

BIBLE STUDY

1. How many books are in the Old Testament? In the New Testament?
2. Adding the numbers, how many books are there in the Bible?
3. John 3:16 is called the heart of the Bible. Learn it.
4. Read II Corinthians 11:23-33.

QUESTIONS

1. What is the good fight of faith?
2. Why should we fight the fight of faith? (Lesson Text.)
3. What did Paul meet in his fight for the faith in Christ? How did he fight?
4. How do we receive Christ? (In Baptism.) When did Paul receive Christ? (See Lesson 25.)
5. How does Baptism make us one with Christ? (Baptism IV and 4th line in Hymn Verse.)
6. How does Satan tempt us? Why does he tempt us?
7. How did Paul keep close to Christ?

Paul Is Taken Prisoner

Chapter 34
CONFESSION

How people should be taught to confess.

QUESTION: What is Confession?

ANSWER: Confession consists of two parts: the one is that we confess our sins; the other, that we receive absolution or forgiveness from the pastor as from God Himself, in no wise doubting, but firmly believing, that our sins are thereby forgiven before God in heaven.

QUESTION: What sins should we confess?

ANSWER: Before God we should acknowledge ourselves guilty of all manner of sins, even of those of which we are not aware, as we do in the Lord's Prayer. To the pastor we should confess only those sins which we know and feel in our hearts.

QUESTION: What are such sins?

ANSWER: Here examine yourself in the light of the Ten Commandments, whether as father or mother, son or daughter, master or servant, you have been disobedient, unfaithful, slothful, ill-tempered, unchaste, or quarrelsome, or whether you have injured any one by word, or deed, stolen, neglected, or wasted aught, or done any other evil.

The Lost Son

THE younger son of a wise and kind father was out in the world at last. Long had he dreamed of this. He had just received his share of the property. Now there was nothing to stop him from doing great things, meeting the right people, making real friends, building a wonderful home, and having a "good time." It was so good to be rid of such drawbacks as father, brother, and home with its rules and regulations. Now he could become the great man that he knew he was meant to be.

He found many friends in the far land who helped him on his chosen road to greatness. Money bought all he had dreamed of except heroic deeds and a happy home. His gay, sinful life took the strength he needed for the deeds, and the riotous "good times" ate up the money that should have built the home.

He grew more reckless every day. One morning he awoke to

find his money all spent and that he was also without a single friend. What a fool he had been! There had been something worthwhile in him, if he had only saved it. In its place he saw disobedience, selfishness, ungratefulness, and, worst of all, a sin-eaten soul.

He thought of going home, home where even the servants lived in comfort and plenty. In his wretched condition he felt that his father would, and rightly too, turn him away.

He found work as a swineherd, but there was famine in the land. He nearly starved to death. He ate, slept, and lived with the pigs.

The Prodigal Son Herds Swine

Can you see him now—once a thoughtless, selfish, gay, rich, strong young man who planned to be great without saving, without obeying, without denying himself, and without taking God into account?

Home haunted him. He found himself whispering his childhood prayers. At last he came to himself. He must go home. He would confess his dreadful sins to his father and ask for a place among the servants. What did it matter if they saw him as the failure he was! All he wanted was his father's forgiving arms around him, no matter what anyone else might think of him.

While he was yet a long way off his father saw him and ran to meet him. What a relief to rest his weary head on that loving breast and sob: *I have sinned against heaven, and in thy sight: I am no more worthy to be called thy son.* The father led him to his old room. He ordered the fatted calf killed for the festal meal. While the feast was being made ready the servants bathed the prodigal, dressed him in the best robe, put shoes on his feet and a ring (the sign of sonship) on his finger. (This story is based on Luke 15:11-24.)

LESSON TEXT

I have sinned against heaven, and in thy sight. Luke 15:18.

HYMN (See page 144)

PRAYER

Teach me to live soberly, righteously, and godly every day. Help me to give the best in me to Thee while I am still young. Amen.

BIBLE STUDY

1. Find the following books in your Bible: Numbers; Judges; Song of Solomon; Lamentations; Daniel; Amos; Malachi.
2. Mary, Jesus' mother, sang a song called Magnificat. It is in Luke 1:46-55. Find it.
3. Read Luke 15:11-24.

QUESTIONS

1. Why did the son want to leave home?
2. What kind of home and father did he have? Prove your answer from the story.
3. Find the places in the story that prove that this father loved his son.
4. What is a "good time"? How did the son try to find it?
5. What does "come to himself" mean? What made him come to himself?
6. What did he see when he came to himself? What did he do?
7. Why did his friends leave him? Why is not *friends* the right name for his companions in sin?
8. What had sin and the world done to him? Can you show that there still was a longing for better things in him?
9. Why was the father to his son as God is to sinner?
10. Was the father satisfied that the confession was sincere? Why?
11. Why should we confess our sins to God?
12. How can we keep from doing what is sin? How can our parents help us? How can our pastor help us if we let him? How can we get God to help us?

The Prodigal Son Returns

Chapter 35

THE SACRAMENT OF THE ALTAR

I

QUESTION: What is the Sacrament of the Altar?

ANSWER: It is the true Body and Blood of our Lord Jesus Christ, under the bread and wine, given unto us Christians to eat and to drink, as it was instituted by Christ Himself.

QUESTION: Where is it so written?

ANSWER: The holy Evangelists, Matthew, Mark, and Luke, together with St. Paul, write thus:

"Our Lord Jesus Christ, in the night in which He was betrayed, took bread; and when He had given thanks, He brake it and gave it to His disciples, saying, Take, eat; this is My Body, which is given for you; this do in remembrance of Me.

"After the same manner, also, He took the cup, when He had supped, and when He had given thanks, He gave it to them, saying, Drink ye all of it; this cup is the New Testament in My Blood, which is shed for you, and for many, for the remission of sins; this do, as oft as ye drink it, in remembrance of Me."

II

QUESTION: What is the benefit of such eating and drinking?

ANSWER: It is pointed out in these words: "Given and shed for you for the remission of sins." Through these words the remission of sins, life and salvation are given unto us in the Sacrament; for where there is remission of sins, there is also life and salvation.

Jesus Institutes the Lord's Supper

THE evening before Jesus was crucified He met with His disciples to eat the Passover. While they waited for the meal to begin the disciples talked about who should be the greatest in the kingdom of God. It seems the talk started because they could not agree who should do the foot-washing. Each thought he was too great and too important to be a servant for the rest.

While they were arguing Jesus arose, removed His outer garment, and tied a towel around His waist and washed the disciples' feet. When He had made the round of them all He said: *The*

The Last Supper

kings of the Gentiles have lordship over them; and they that have authority over them are called benefactors. But ye shall not be so.... For which is greater, he that sitteth at meat, or he that serveth? is not he that sitteth at meat? but I am in the midst of you as He that serveth.

Then they understood why Jesus acted as their servant. The important question was not who stood first in the church but who was willing to be a servant like Jesus.

Jesus sat at the head of the table. He told His disciples He wanted to eat this Passover with them before He suffered. He thought of them and also of His future disciples. He wanted to give them another means of grace whereby He could meet them after He had gone to heaven. Jesus offered a prayer and the meal began.

During the meal Jesus took the bread, blessed it, brake it, and gave it to them, saying, *Take, eat; this is My body.* Then He took the cup, gave thanks, and gave it to them, saying, *Drink ye all of it; for this is My blood of the covenant, which is poured out for many unto remission of sins.*

Jesus poured out to them what was in His heart. He spoke to them of His Father's house, about His coming back to them, and added that He had many things to tell them, but would not, because they could not understand them now. He comforted them by saying, *The Holy Spirit, whom the Father will send in my name, He shall teach you all things, and bring to your remembrance all that I said unto you.*

Then they all sang another psalm (they had sung several during the meal) and went out into the night to the silent garden of Gethsemane. (This story is based on Luke 22:7-30.)

LESSON TEXT

Take, eat; this my body. . . . Drink ye all of it; for this is my blood of the covenant, which is poured out for many unto remission of sins. Matthew 26:26-27.

HYMN (See page 144)

PRAYER

I thank Thee, Lord Jesus, for the many ways by which Thou hast revealed Thy love to us. Help me to make the right use of Thy means of grace so I may always remain Thy humble and faithful disciple. Amen.

BIBLE STUDY

1. Find the following books in your Bible: Joshua; II Samuel; Ezra; Esther; Ecclesiastes; Zephaniah; Zechariah; Mark; Colossians; I Timothy; Philemon.
2. Find the Shepherd Psalm. (See Bible Study, Chapter 29.) Repeat it.

QUESTIONS

1. What did the disciples do when they came into the room? (Luke 22:24.)
2. Why did Jesus wash the disciples' feet? (Lesson 20 and Luke 22:26, 27.)
3. How did they feel when Jesus waited on them? Why?
4. What did Jesus do before they ate?
5. Jesus loved His disciples. Find places in the story that prove it.
6. What does the Lord's Supper give us? (See Lesson Text.)

Chapter 36
THE SACRAMENT OF THE ALTAR

III

Question: How can the bodily eating and drinking produce such great benefits?

Answer: The eating and drinking, indeed, do not produce them, but the words: "Given and shed for you for the remission of sins." For besides the bodily eating and drinking, these words are the chief thing in the Sacrament; and he who believes them has what they say and declare, namely, the remission of sins.

IV

Question: Who, then, receives the Sacrament worthily?

Answer: Fasting and bodily preparation are indeed a good outward discipline, but he is truly worthy and well prepared who believes these words: "Given and shed for you for the remission of sins." But he who does not believe these words or who doubts them is unworthy and unprepared; for the words: "For you," require truly believing hearts.

Early Christians at the Lord's Supper

THE early Christians at Jerusalem worshipped God in the temple. But they also went to special meetings that were held in the homes throughout the city. There were no large buildings or halls where they could meet. Their services were much like ours, made up of singing, praying, preaching, and partaking of the Lord's Supper.

These meetings were happy ones because Christ was with them although they could not see Him. Their reason for coming together was to be with Him as a group. Besides, they found strength in being together with those who loved Jesus. *They took their food with gladness and singleness of heart, praising God, and having favor with all the people.*

Jesus' words, *This do, as often as ye drink it, in remembrance of Me,* mean that we should come to the Lord's Supper often. This the early Christians did. They celebrated the Lord's Supper every day. It was called the breaking of bread. Later they had it only on Sunday, the day when the congregation came together as a group, especially at the evening service. In Corinth this evening meal was a love feast. Everyone brought something for the meal which they ate together in the name of their Lord.

It was a feast of joy. They were yet so near to Christ's presence on earth that they felt He was with them as their host and they were His guests. Then came a time when they seemed to forget the meaning of the Lord's Supper and brought more and richer foods and drink to the love feast. They seemed to enjoy the eating and drinking more than they did their fellowship in Christ. This was especially true among the Christians at Corinth.

Paul was in Ephesus when he heard about this disorderly practice. He wrote them a letter about this and other matters. The letter is Paul's First Epistle to the Corinthians, from which this lesson is taken. He reminded them of what Jesus had said at the first Lord's Supper. Paul said that to take the body and blood of Christ as ordinary food is sin.

At the Lord's Table we meet Christ. He is the Host, we are His guests. It is a love feast at which Jesus is present to give Himself to us. (This story is based on I Corinthians 10:16-17.)

LESSON TEXT

We, who are many, are one bread, one body: for we all partake of the one bread. I Corinthians 10:17.

HYMN (See page 144)

PRAYER

Keep us faithful, keep us pure,
Keep as evermore Thine own;
Help, O help us to endure;
Fit us for the promised crown.

BIBLE STUDY

Read Isaiah 53. It is a prophecy of the suffering and death of Jesus, the Messiah.

QUESTIONS

1. Where did the early Christians meet? Why?
2. Who made up their congregations?
3. In what ways were their meetings like ours? How different?
4. Why were their meetings joyous affairs?

5. Find the part in the story that tells us they were worthy of the Lord's Supper.
6. Why did Paul write to the congregation in Corinth? What did he tell them to do? (Find this letter in the Bible.)
7. What does the Lesson Text mean? (The bread is Christ. He makes us all one in Himself.)
8. What does the Lord's Supper give us? (See Catechism.)
9. Be sure you can say Parts III and IV of the Catechism from memory.

Hymns

(Abbreviations—C.: The Concordia Hymnal; L. H.: The Lutheran Hymnary.)

CHAPTER 1 (C. No. 91)

God's Word is our great heritage,
And shall be ours forever;
To spread its light from age to age
Shall be our chief endeavor;
Through life it guides our way,
In death it is our stay;
Lord grant, while worlds endure,
We keep its teachings pure,
Throughout all generations. Amen.

CHAPTER 2 (C. No. 19, vs. 1 and 3)

My God, how wonderful Thou art,
Thy majesty how bright!
How beautiful Thy mercy-seat
In depths of burning light!
How wonderful, how beautiful,
The sight of Thee must be,
Thine endless wisdom, boundless power,
And awful purity! Amen.

CHAPTER 3 (C. No. 144, vs. 1 and 2)

Jesus, name of wondrous love,
Name all other names above!
Unto which must ev'ry knee
Bow in deep humility.
Jesus, name of priceless worth
To the fallen sons of earth,
For the promise that it gave,
"Jesus shall His people save." Amen.

CHAPTER 4 (C. No. 44, v. 1)

O day of rest and gladness,
O day of joy and light,
O balm of care and sadness,
Most beautiful, most bright,
On thee, the high and lowly
Through ages joined in tune,
Sing Holy, Holy, Holy!
To the great God Triune. Amen.

CHAPTER 5 (C. No. 364, v. 2)

I'm glad my blessed Savior
Was once a child like me,
To show how pure and holy
His little ones should be;
And if I try to follow
His holy footsteps here below,
He never will forget me,
Because He loves me so. Amen.

CHAPTER 6 (C. No. 320, vs. 1 and 4)

O that the Lord would guide my ways,
To keep His statutes still!
O that my God would grant me grace
To know and do His will!
Make me to walk in Thy commands;
'Tis a delightful road:
Nor let my head or heart or hands
Offend against my God. Amen.

CHAPTER 7 (C. No. 270, v. 1)

When sinners see their lost condition,
And feel the pressing load of sin,
And Jesus cometh on His mission
To heal the sin-sick heart within,
All grief must flee before His grace,
And joy divine will take its place. Amen.

CHAPTER 8 (C. No. 406, vs. 1 and 4)

Take my life and let it be
Consecrated, Lord, to Thee;
Take my moments and my days,
Let them flow in ceaseless praise.
Take my silver and my gold,
Not a mite would I withhold;
Take my intellect, and use
Ev'ry pow'r as Thou dost choose. Amen.

CHAPTER 9 (C. No. 379, v. 1)

How shall the young secure their hearts,   Thy Word the choicest rules imparts
And guard their lives from sin?   To keep the conscience clean. Amen.

CHAPTER 10 (C. No. 406, v. 4)

Take my silver and my gold,   Take my intellect, and use
Not a mite would I withhold;   Ev'ry pow'r as Thou dost choose. Amen.

CHAPTER 11 (L. H. No. 46, v. 1)

How blest are they who hear God's Word,   Their light shines brighter day by day,
And keep and heed what they have heard: And while they tread life's weary way,
And wisdom daily gather;   They have the oil of gladness
    To soothe their pain and sadness. Amen.

CHAPTER 12 (C. No. 19, v. 7)

My God, how wonderful Thou art,   On Thee I stay my trusting heart,
Thou everlasting Friend!   Till faith in vision end. Amen.

CHAPTER 13 (C. No. 16, v. 1)

Thee, God, we praise, Thy name we bless,   The whole creation worships Thee,
Thee, Lord of all, we do confess;   The Father of eternity. Amen.

CHAPTER 14 (C. No. 370, v. 2)

Our fathers, chained in prisons dark,   If they, like them, should die for Thee:
Were still in heart and conscience free;   Faith of our fathers, holy faith,
And blest would be their children's fate   We will be true to thee till death. Amen.

CHAPTER 15 (C. No. 140, v. 2)

Silent night! Holy night!   "Hallelujah! Hail the King!
Darkness flies, and all is light!   Jesus the Savior is here!
Shepherds hear the angels sing   Jesus the Savior is here!" Amen.

CHAPTER 16 (C. No. 57, vs. 2 and 3)

Abide, Lord, with the story   Abide, our pathway brighten
Of Thy redeeming love;   With Thy celestial ray;
May we the Gospel's glory   Blest light, our souls enlighten,
And saving virtue prove.   Show us the truth, the way. Amen.

CHAPTER 17 (C. No. 189, v. 1)

'Tis finished! So the Savior cried,   'Tis finished! Yes, the race is run,
And meekly bowed His head and died: The battle fought, the vict'ry won. Amen.

CHAPTER 18 (C. No. 198, v. 3)

Three days of weeping quickly sped;   Glory to Him, our risen Head!
Glorious He rises from the dead;   Alleluia. Amen.

CHAPTER 19 (C. No. 53, v. 1)

O Holy Spirit, enter in,   Around and in us brightly shine,
And in our hearts Thy work begin,   To joy and gladness wake us.
Thy temple deign to make us;   That we to Thee truly living,
Sun of the soul,   To Thee giving pray'r unceasing,
Thou Light divine,   Still may be in love increasing. Amen.

CHAPTER 20 (C. No. 19, v. 6)
No earthly father loves like Thee,
No mother e'er so mild,

Bears and forbears, as Thou hast done
With me, Thy sinful child. Amen.

CHAPTER 21 (C. No. 422, v. 3)
As rises from the ocean
The sun in bright array
With beauty for its portion
To lead the new-born day,

So shall I rise all glorious
His crowned bride to be
Who rose o'er death victorious,
To share His life with me. Amen.

CHAPTER 22 (C. No. 11, v. 1)
Sweet hour of prayer, sweet hour of prayer!
That calls me from a world of care,
And bids me at my Father's throne
Make all my wants and wishes known:

In seasons of distress and grief,
My soul has often found relief;
And oft escaped the tempter's snare,
By thy return, sweet hour of prayer!
       Amen.

CHAPTER 23 (C. No. 374, v. 1)
Onward, Christian soldiers,
Marching as to war,
With the cross of Jesus
Going on before:
Christ, the royal Master,
Leads against the foe;
Forward into battle,
See, His banners go.

CHORUS:

Onward, Christian soldiers,
Marching as to war,
With the cross of Jesus
Going on before. Amen.

CHAPTER 24 (L. H. No. 260, v. 4)
Precious Jesus, I beseech Thee:
May Thy words take root in me;
May this gift from heaven enrich me,
So that I bear fruit for Thee;

Take them never from my heart,
Till I see Thee as Thou art,
When in heavenly bliss and glory,
I shall see Thee and adore Thee. Amen.

CHAPTER 25 (C. No. 156, v. 1)
My Jesus, as Thou wilt!
O may Thy will be mine;
Into Thy hand of love
I would my all resign.

Through sorrow, or through joy,
Conduct me as Thine own,
And help me still to say,
My Lord, Thy will be done! Amen.

CHAPTER 26 (C. 409, v. 1)
Go, labor on: spend and be spent,
Thy joy to do the Father's will;

It is the way the Master went;
Should not the servant tread it still?
       Amen.

CHAPTER 27 (L. H. No. 491, v. 2)
That martyr first, whose eagle eye
Could pierce beyond the grave;
Who saw his Master in the sky,
And called on Him to save;

Like Him, with pardon on His tongue,
In midst of mortal pain,
He prayed for them that did the wrong:
Who follows in His train? Amen.

CHAPTER 28 (L. H. No. 430, v. 8)
Be on your guard,
Keep watch and ward.*
Beware of Satan's cunning!

Watch and pray and trust your Lord.
Till ye see Him coming. Amen.

*Ward means guard.

CHAPTER 29 (C. No. 286, v. 2)
In His presence I am safe,
Naught can me encumber.
He is watching night and day,
He will never slumber.

He's my refuge and my strength
And my Father tender,
In temptations and in strife
He is my defender. Amen.

CHAPTER 30 (C. No. 6, v. 4)
Beautiful Savior!
Lord of the nations!
Son of God and Son of Man!

Glory and honor,
Praise, adoration,
Now and forevermore be Thine! Amen.

CHAPTER 31 (C. No. 95, vs. 1-2)
Abide among us, we implore Thee,
Lord Jesus Christ, Thy Spirit breathe!
And let the babes we bring before Thee
Now be baptized into Thy death.

Lord, after Thee we Christians call them,
O let them in Thy name arise!
And keep them Thine whate'er befall them,
That they may reach Thy Paradise. Amen.

CHAPTER 32 (C. No. 94, v. 1)
He that believes and is baptized
Shall see the Lord's salvation;
Baptized into the death of Christ,
He is a new creation;

Through Christ's redemption he shall stand
Among the glorious heav'nly band
Of every tribe and nation. Amen.

CHAPTER 33 (C. No. 94, v. 2)
With one accord, O God, we pray:
Grant us Thy Holy Spirit;
Look Thou on our infirmity
Through Jesus' blood and merit!

Grant us to grow in grace each day
By holy baptism that we may
Eternal life inherit! Amen.

CHAPTER 34 (C. No. 351, v. 4)
O happy home, where Thou art not forgotten
When joy is overflowing, full and free,

O happy home, where every wounded spirit
Is brought, Physician, Comforter, to Thee. Amen.

CHAPTER 35 (C. No. 102, v. 2)
Thy body, broken for my sake,
My bread from heaven shall be;

Thy testamental cup I take,
And thus remember Thee. Amen.

CHAPTER 36 (C. No. 366, v. 8)
We gather 'round Thee, Jesus dear,
So happy in Thy presence here;

Grant us, our Savior, every one,
To stand in heaven before Thy throne. Amen.